FRANCIS BARLOW

EDWARD HODNETT

FRANCIS BARLOW
First Master of
English Book Illustration

UNIVERSITY OF CALIFORNIA PRESS
1978

Printed in Great Britain by
The Scolar Press Ltd
Ilkley, Yorkshire

© Edward Hodnett 1978

ISBN 0-520-93409-0

Library of Congress Catalog Card No. 76-55570

CONTENTS

5

For
ALLISON
with love

The justification of a book about Francis Barlow is that there should be one and there is none. My interest in English book illustration led me to begin to study Barlow in 1967, and it is in the context of the history of English book illustration that I deal with him here. But Barlow cannot be approached in the usual manner. His reputation as an illustrator rests on only two books, but they are major works. His etchings for *Theophila* (1652), a book of religious verse, are unique. On the other hand his illustrations for *Aesop's Fables* (1666, 1687), though of great distinction, are the culmination of a major tradition of Aesopic fable illustration in Europe and associate him so intimately with three of his predecessors, Marcus Gheeraerts the elder, Francis Cleyn, and Wenceslaus Hollar, that it is impossible to discuss his work without discussing theirs. This is the more inescapable because the four are virtually the only significant known interpretive illustrators of the sixteenth and seventeenth centuries in England. Furthermore, by an extraordinary coincidence all four are etchers.

I have used the adjective interpretive throughout in order to avoid misunderstanding. (The spelling interpretive seems to have become an acceptable alternative to the stuttering interpretative still preferred by some purists.) I do so to make clear that I am mainly concerned with designs that convey visual equivalents of scenes in imaginative literature. The artist is then also engaged in a creative act, which can range from mechanical representation to imaginative statements that may be even more illuminating or moving than the words illustrated. As a matter of course interpretive illustrations normally occur in works of *belles-lettres* and record interaction between human or animal characters or between them and their environment.

The success of an interpretive illustration is therefore inextricably related to the text. It cannot be judged as an independent work of art in the same way as portraits and architectural, topographical, botanical, and similar expository designs, which are really prints that are sometimes bound between covers. Although this distinction seems a critical truism, in fact writers about book illustrations usually judge them either solely as if they were prints or as decorative units of the book as a work of art. Since the interpretive function of the illustrator is the standard one, it is time for book illustration to play a larger part in literary scholarship, perhaps as an interdisciplinary study between art and literature.

Etching and engraving are the media used in all of the seventeenth-century books discussed here; therefore a few remarks about them may be useful. For an explanation of the graphic processes one should consult *How Prints Look* by W. M. Ivins, Jr. or a similar book. Engraving came to be preferred to woodcuts in the second half of the sixteenth century because it was a faster, more precise, alterable, and more elegant way of making multiple copies of a drawing. Etching, though not so popular, had the same advantages. As book illustrations, however, engravings and etchings had the disadvantage of having to be printed separately from the letterpress and were more expensive than woodcuts. Therefore they were not used so freely as woodcuts had been – in fact, etchings have never been a common method of illustrating books. In his history of the printing house of Plantin-Moretus, Voet says that illustrations were often 75 per cent of the cost of a book.

A source of confusion in writings about sixteenth- and seventeenth-century illustrations is the distinction between etchings and engravings. As Ivins and other authorities are the first to grant, the distinction in specific instances is not always clear even to the expert; to the uninitiated it rarely is. Until Rembrandt introduced the sort of tonal effects with which we are familiar by stopping out some lines and re-biting others and by leaving some ink on the plate surface, etchings were usually bitten once and then, if necessary, worked over with a burin for strengthening some of the lines. At other times designs were engraved in outline first and then etched. And it was not uncommon to etch one part of a plate – the figures and foliage, say – and engrave another, especially the architecture and parallel-line shading. A second reason for confusion is that some writers and cataloguers, even that distinguished authority A. M. Hind, have unfortunately used the term engraving to cover both methods. I shall keep the difference clear because it is an important one in Barlow's work.

The correct identification of the artist who made the original drawings for illustrations is of prime importance. Cataloguers and writers about prints sometimes credit men who sign plates with illustrating books when they have only etched or engraved another artist's designs. Barlow and Gheeraerts have both suffered in this way. This confusion arises from the habit of early reproductive etchers and engravers frequently signing their own names to plates and ignoring the artist. (They were commonly paid more than he was.) It is of crucial importance to recognize that, except in those rare instances where we have the original drawings to compare with the plates, our judgments on all etched or engraved illustrations are subject to gross miscalculations. For instance, when Hollar does the etching of a Barlow drawing, the close resemblance to the rest of Hollar's work tells us that we are looking at a somewhat refined, tightened-up version of the original. When a journeyman takes over the etching, we have to remember that we may be looking at the original as though on a maladjusted television screen.

A common source of critical blindness is the difficulty of imagining that a fine drawing can have been the model for a poor plate. Or our judgment may suffer from a certain ambivalence. If we are trying to account for the work of individual artists and we are acquainted with their own 'hands', we naturally imagine what the original drawings underlying the etchings or engravings were like. If, on the other hand, we are concerned with the act of book illustration, we should, no doubt, judge only what readers see. This perplexity exists to some extent whether or not an artist is his own etcher or engraver. An artist – Francis Cleyn is an example – can be an accomplished draughtsman and an indifferent etcher or engraver. But etchings and engravings, no matter how well they are done, are inevitably different from the pencil, pen, and wash drawings on which they are based. The only things that remain constant, though the effects may change, are the artists' concepts drawn from the text or borrowed from earlier illustrations.

*   *   *   *   *

As always, my debt to the writers of the books listed in the Bibliography – and the friends who are not – is great. All students of Barlow owe much to Walter Shaw Sparrow's enthusiastic writing forty and fifty years ago about Barlow's etching, particularly his sporting prints. For help in specific matters I am happy to express my thanks to Mr. Paul Hulton and Mr. Peter Moore of the Department of Prints and Drawings of the British Museum, Mr. John de Wit of the Ashmolean Museum, Oxford, Mr. David L. Paisey and Mr. Peter C. Hogg of the British Library, Dr. Hans-Joachim Zimmermann and Dr. Margret Schuchard of Heidelberg University, Mr. Richard T. Godfrey of the Colchester School of Art, and Mr. Martin Bailey of the Scolar Press. No one who has enjoyed the hospitality of the North Library of the British Library for the years that I have can be anything but profoundly grateful to the staff for their unfailing efficiency and friendliness. And the least I can do is to say thank you to the member of my family who has patiently typed my manuscript and listened to monologues about Barlow on our walks in Hyde Park. Thank you, Jessie.

EDWARD HODNETT *London September* 1975

CHAPTER I

Francis Barlow's Career

Francis Barlow (1626?–1704) is the first native English book illustrator –
indeed, the leading interpretive illustrator in England before 1800 and one
of the masters in nearly five centuries of English book illustration. He is also the
first professional English etcher, the first and one of the best of English animal
and bird draughtsmen, the first English artist to record sporting scenes, in prints,
book illustrations, and paintings, and the first important English political car-
toonist. In *Tudor and Stuart Drawings* Woodward says he 'could also, with equal
justice, qualify as the first English landscape artist'. Admittedly Barlow's place as
an etcher and painter depends largely on his subjects and his primacy in time: he
used both etching and oil-painting essentially as media for reproducing his drawings. This book is mainly concerned with his work as an interpretive illustrator.

Francis Barlow was first of all a splendid draughtsman who found book illustration congenial. Otto Benesch of the Albertina Museum, Vienna, has called him
'one of the greatest illustrators of all time'. This estimate may be surprising, but
Benesch was one of the most authoritative art historians of the period and one
who thought more broadly than most about book illustration. Let us say that
Barlow's illustrative work is sufficiently substantial and memorable to give him a
place beside Thomas Rowlandson, William Blake, George Cruikshank, John
Martin, Edward Burne-Jones, Aubrey Beardsley, and a few other distinguished
British interpreters of imaginative literature.

As we shall see in Chapter II, the best illustrations in books printed in England
before Barlow are importations or copies of foreign designs, or they are the work
of foreign-born artists or anonymous but probably foreign-born artists. William
Faithorne is the only known English artist besides Barlow who might be called a
book illustrator before 1700, but his title is not easy to certify. Whatever the
merits of portraits, ornamental frontispieces and title-pages, maps, and architectural designs, native engravers like Rogers, Hole, Cecill, Payne, Marshall, and
Robert White are book decorators, not illustrators in the customary sense used
here. Indeed, only three known foreign artists resident in England can be con-

sidered Barlow's predecessors as significant book illustrators – Marcus Gheer-aerts the elder, Francis Cleyn, and Wenceslaus Hollar. Their work is closely associated with his and will be discussed in later chapters.

Contemporary References by Symonds and Evelyn

The '1648' on a signed drawing of David slaying the lion is the first firm date we can assign to Barlow. In 1650 he was elected a member of the Painter-Stainers Company, which normally required an apprenticeship of seven years beginning at fifteen. He would therefore have been born in 1628, but perhaps the reported 1626 is correct. In 1652 he illustrated his first book, Benlowes' *Theophila*, and emerged from obscurity as a full-fledged master. The earliest dated personal reference to him occurs in one of Richard Symonds' little notebooks in the Manuscript Room of the British Museum (*Egerton MSS 1636). The antiquarian dated a visit to look at paintings at Arundel House in the Strand 1653. Apparently not long afterwards he filled a page in his minuscular hand with notes of an interview with Barlow. What the artist told him about the colours he used for portraits, fish, ducks, and landscapes is not enlightening. Nevertheless, the notes contain informative details. At the top of the page Symonds writes, 'Barlow living neare ye Drum in Drury Lane'. That Symonds, who had just returned from gathering information about painting in Italy, considered Barlow worth interviewing suggests a certain standing. Then in one of his notes Symonds says: 'For a quadro [a painting on board or canvas on a frame] of ffishes he made he had 8 l^i [pounds]. He uses to make fowle and birds and colour them from the life.' This makes it seem probable that, as we shall infer later, young Barlow has been in London working at his profession, not soldiering and not in exile. The considerable sum in Cromwell's Commonwealth of £8 for a painting of a fish confirms the impression that he has attained a solid reputation.

Next in John Evelyn's *Diary* for 16 February 1656 we read 'Went with Dr. Wilkins to see Barlow the famous Paynter of fowle Beastes & Birds'. By the age of thirty he must have accomplished a good deal for the restrained Evelyn to use 'famous' so matter-of-factly. Yet in the same year Barlow was not too proud to make a modest drawing of a master carpenter as a frontispiece for a humble little manual of carpentry. Then three days before Christmas Barlow and a fellow etcher, Richard Gaywood, having a copy of one of Titian's paintings of Venus with an organist, dedicated it to Evelyn, and sent it to him 'From the Black Boy over against St. Dunstan's Fleet-street', Henry Seile's bookshop. Barlow concludes his accompanying note: 'A[s] eaching is not my profefsion, I hope you will not expect much from me. Sir, if you shall be pleased to honner my weake, yet willing endeavours with your exseptation, I shall ever rest obliged for this and former favours'. Whatever Barlow and Gaywood hoped to get in return for their not negligible Christmas gift, they were disappointed. Though genuinely interested in art and affluent enough to reward the 'famous painter' he had gone to see in February, Evelyn replied the next day at length with mealy-mouthed evasions, including 'If I had known of your design, you should on my advice have nuncupated this handsome monument of your skill and dexterity to some great one'.

Vertue's Account

We get our first comprehensive account of Barlow and his work from the engraver and would-be art historian George Vertue (1684–1756), who was an assistant of the engraver Michael van der Gucht while Barlow was still alive and who must have talked to many people who had known Barlow. He also had access to Symonds' notes and used the ones we have quoted. The following quotations from the dozen or so scattered entries in Vertue's *Note Books*, published from the manuscripts in the British Museum by the Walpole Society, are the most helpful of the early references:

> several prints drawn & Etch'd. by . . . Barlow. with the picture of Ed. Benlow Esq in fol. for this book of Divine Poems. Theophila. printed 1652 by this it appears that Barlow was then a man of some fame. or reputation. the Animals that are etched are done with Spirit. & judgement. (ii, 72)

> Francis Barlow, was born in Lincolnshire & at his coming to London, put prentice to one Shepherd, a Face-Painter, with whom he liv'd but a few years because his fancy did not lye that way, his Genious leading him wholly to drawing of Fowl, Fish and Beasts, wherein he arriv'd to that Perfection, that had his Colouring & Pencilling been as good as his Draught; which was most exact, he might have easily excell'd all that went before him in that kind of Painting, of which we have an Instance in the six books of Prints after him. He drew some Ceilings of Birds for Noblemen & Gentlemen in the Country. There are several Prints extant after the Designs of this Master, Among which are the Cutts for a new Edition of Aesop's Fables, in which Undertaking he wanted due Encoragement. He also drew several of the Monuments in Westminster-Abby, & in Henry VII's Chappel, which were intended for a Large Edition of Mr Keep's Monumenta Westmonasteriencia. But notwithstanding all Mr Barlows Excellency in his way, & tho' he had the good Fortune to have a considerable Sum of Money left him by a Friend, he died poor in the year 1702. (ii, 135–6)

We must be grateful to Vertue for his immense industry in collecting raw materials for the work he never wrote, but we cannot accept as fact any data not corroborated from other sources. For instance, Vertue was not so certain about the death date of Barlow as he seems to be, for he made a note to himself: 'Mr. Barlow painter died at Westminster. inquire at the Robin Hood on the Mill bank. Le Mense'. (i, 65) He seems more certain that the artist was born in Lincolnshire. Redgrave gives the exact date 1626 with no supporting authority. D. M. K. Marendaz, writing about the painting 'The Decoy Pond at Sunset', says that the landscape is typical of East Anglia and adds: 'Barlow was born in Lincolnshire, the precise place I have been unable so far to trace. It is only in such country that the decoying of wild birds can be practised.' Alas for *only*. The scene was in Surrey. And a topographical print in Stow and Strype's *A Survey of London and Westminster* (1720) shows a decoy in St. James' Park. On the title-page of his *Multae et diversae Avium Species* the artist goes out of his way to say 'per Franciscum Barlovium Anglum . . . Indigenam Londoninensem'. That does not settle the question either.

William Shepherd (Sheppard) (*fl. c.* 1665), Barlow's master and a member of the Painter-Stainers Company, is remembered chiefly for a full-length portrait of the playwright Thomas Killigrew painted in Venice in 1650. (One copy is now at Woburn Abbey.) Vertue's remark that Barlow left Shepherd after a few years because he preferred painting birds, animals, and fish to doing portraits of human beings raises two questions. Theoretically Barlow would have had to finish his seven years with another master. Did he? And from whom did he learn to etch? For an engraver writing a history of painting and engraving, Vertue has nothing much to say about Barlow as an etcher. Nor has Evelyn in *Sculptura*.

Sparrow suggests that Francis Cleyn might have been Barlow's etching teacher. At the probable time, the mid-1640s, Cleyn could have taught Barlow the mechanics of etching, but he is so inferior in this medium that one tends to reject him and to look for someone who could have inspired Barlow. The two artists who meet this condition are Anthony van Dyck and Wenceslaus Hollar. Van Dyck established an atelier in Blackfriars in 1632, but his known etchings were made earlier in Antwerp, and he died in 1641. Only through his prints or an assistant could he have influenced Barlow. Between 1636 and 1645 Hollar was in London. He taught Richard Gaywood and Thomas Dudley and influenced Francis Place, all associated with Barlow. He would seem the most logical person to teach Barlow. Yet if he had, we can be certain that the fact would be well known and reported. Jan Baptist Gaspars (see Chapter II) is said to have come to London from Antwerp in the 1640s. Barlow might have known him. About all that we can say with certainty is that Barlow's loose technique is in the style of Van Dyck's etched portraits in *Iconographie* and of Gaspar's *Extravagant Shepherd* illustrations, and does not resemble Hollar's at all.

The Golden Eagle on New Street near Shoe Lane

Sometime between 1653 and 1665 Barlow moved from Drury Lane to New Street, half way between Fleet Street and Holborn. The engraved title-page of his Aesop says the book is to be sold 'at his House The Golden Eagle in New Street near Shoo-Lane'. The last phrase suggests that the house was on Little New Street, the short stretch from Shoe Lane to New Square, from which an angular section, now Harding Street, connects with Fetter Lane. 'At his House' disposes of Sparrow's suggestion that The Golden Eagle was a bookseller's shop, not Barlow's residence. Holborn Viaduct and large post-war office buildings have completely changed the area above New Street and New Square, but the pattern of streets, passages, courts, and squares and the size of most of the buildings below New Street – indeed, along all of Fleet Street from Temple Bar to Ludgate Circus and in all of Whitefriars and the Temple between Fleet Street and the Thames – is not so changed that we cannot imagine what it was like in Barlow's time.

Two facts about the Fleet Street area are worth remembering in relation to Barlow. Ever since Pynson, De Worde, and Notary moved their presses there about 1500, it had been the chief centre for printing and allied trades in London. During a career of half a century Barlow must have become acquainted not only with most of the printers, artists, engravers, booksellers, and printsellers but also with a large number of writers, lawyers, philosophers, scientists, politicians, and leaders of society who lived nearby or frequented the numerous coffee houses and taverns along the three-quarters of a mile from Drury Lane to St. Paul's.

In the hot summer of 1665 Shoe Lane had perhaps the first case of the plague (apparently no worse than the one in 1630), and then on 6 September 1666 the Fire of London in its last day crossed Shoe Lane and New Street, burning down The Golden Eagle, and stopped just short of Temple Bar. Where Barlow lived for the next thirty-eight years is unknown, but his record of continued employment makes it probable that he stayed in the neighbourhood and not unlikely that he rebuilt his house as others did. But Vertue says he died in Westminster, and his memorandum about making inquiries suggests that Barlow may have been living in the Millbank area, near the Tate Gallery, that is.

Vertue says that Barlow died in poverty. Since this is the period of his life that Vertue's informants must have known best, the statement is doubtless true. In 1702 the Earl of Bristol paid Barlow £35, now equal to many times that amount, for paintings by 'Carlotto and Guido' – *i.e.*, Carlo Dolci or Carlo Maratti and Guido Reni, according to Croft-Murray and Hulton. That Barlow owned at least two works of art of this value in 1702 suggests that he may have been reasonably affluent but was raising money to pay for the reissue of his fable book in 1703. Sparrow found that he was buried in the churchyard of St. Margaret's, Westminster, 11 August 1704, as 'Mr. Fra: Barlow, Limner'. The term 'limner' variously meant an illuminator, a portraitist, and a miniaturist, none of which seems to fit Barlow.

Patrons

In accordance with custom from Caxton to Dr. Johnson, Barlow is said to have sought patronage from at least five wealthy men besides Evelyn. They were Sir Francis Prujean, M.D., General George Monk, the first Earl of Albemarle, William Cavendish, the fourth Earl of Devonshire, Denzil Onslow, and John Hervey, the first Earl of Bristol. He also worked for the Duke of Lauderdale and dedicated prints to other potential patrons. In what measure these eminent men rewarded Barlow with money, hospitality, influence, or friendship is not known, but the evidence suggests that they were more generous than Evelyn. His association with them throws some light on his career.

Sir Francis Prujean (1591–1665/6) apparently grew up in Boothby, Lincolnshire, and after finishing his medical studies at Cambridge practised in Lincolnshire from 1625 to 1638. In London he became a man of importance in medical circles, was knighted by Charles II on 1 April 1661, and attended Queen Catherine when she was ill with typhus in 1663. Luckily she recovered. Evelyn visited him – 'that famous Physitian' – on 14 August 1661 to see not only his laboratory and workshop but also his pictures and to hear him play on the 'polyphone', a harp-like instrument. To have him turn to Dr. Prujean lends credence to Vertue's statement that Barlow also came from Lincolnshire.

The politic General George Monk (1608–1670) was well rewarded by Charles II by more than the title of first Duke of Albemarle for engineering the Restoration with no conditions. As the man in charge of London during the Great Plague and the Great Fire, he might have been of special help to Barlow in those difficult times. Barlow painted his portrait and designed the elaborate hearse for his interment in Westminster Abbey (1670).

William Cavendish (1640–1707) became fourth Earl of Devonshire in 1684 and first Duke in 1694. He was one of the moderate leaders in anti-Catholic activities during the reign of Charles II and in the secret negotiations that brought William of Orange to the throne. Barlow's dedication to him of the second edition of *Aesop's Fables* (1687) refers to 'Your Lordships many Favours towards me'. Since he had been in the midst of the investigations of the Popish Plot, he may have been responsible for Barlow's involvement with that unhappy episode. He may also have taken an interest in Barlow because he was 'addicted to sport'. He was a generous man with scholarly hobbies, and he was the builder of Chatsworth. Barlow designed his bookplate, his coat of arms.

The relation between Barlow and the wealthy Denzil Onslow is the clearest. Onslow lived grandly among the 'pleasures & inventions' of the manor he bought in 1677 at Pyrford, Surrey, 23 miles from London on the River Wey. In recording a memorable feast that he enjoyed there in August 1681, Evelyn observes that it was all provided by the estate: 'Venison, Rabbts, hairs, Pheasants, Partridge, pigeons, Quaile, Poultrie, all sorts of fowle in season (from his owne Decoy neere his house) all sorts of fresh fish . . . After dinner we went to see sport at the decoy, I never saw so many herons &c . . . The howse is Timber . . . the hall adorned with paintings of fowle, & huntings &c: the work of Mr Barlow who is excellent in this kind from life.' The house was torn down in 1776, but four of the Pyrford paintings, together with two others by Barlow, survive at Clandon Park, Lord Onslow's estate near Guildford, Surrey.

John Hervey (1665–1751), Baron Hervey of Ickworth (1703), first Earl of Bristol (1714), married two heiresses, the second being a lady of the bedchamber to Queen Catherine, though he was a Whig. In the words of the *Dictionary of National Biography*, Hervey was 'a very amiable man and an accomplished scholar' as well as 'a great sportsman, lover of Horse-matches and play', likely grounds for his interest in Barlow.

His Paintings

This is a good place to mention some of Barlow's paintings because in them we can see what must have been his guiding force as an artist and one that underlies much of his work as an illustrator.

Among the Onslow paintings at Clandon Park are one of a dozen or so birds enjoying a haul of fish lying on the ground (signed and dated 1667, ten years before Denzil Onslow came to Pyrford); a farmyard with pheasants, chickens, turkeys, and a boar in a sty; and particularly interesting, what must be the Pyrford decoy, a hut and a net across a narrow piece of water, doubtless the Wey, with nearly four dozen birds of all sorts on the ground and in the air. These three Clandon paintings are astonishingly large, about 9 × 13 feet. A frieze of some fourteen dogs of a mixed breed called southern-mouthed hounds is 12 feet long. In *British Sporting Artists* W. S. Sparrow reproduces these paintings in monochrome. He also reproduces in colour one of a man shooting plover. The colours are mostly subdued burnt sienna, gold, and green. It is from the collection of E. D. Tyrwhitt-Drake formerly at 'Shardeloes' near Amersham. A painting of a carp and large pike in the same collection seems to be dated 1696.

In the face of the pro-foreign policy of the Restoration court, it was a mark of respect for Barlow to be the only English artist chosen to work beside painters like Hendrik Danckerts, Jan Griffier, and Willem van de Velde the younger on the redecoration of Ham House by the Duke and Duchess of Lauderdale. Barlow painted birds on a pair of overdoors. One is damaged but signed and dated 1673. The other shows an owl sitting in a hole of a tree stoically accepting the abuse of a handsome assortment of smaller birds (Waterhouse, pl. 74). John Maitland (1616–1682), a tough Scot Covenanter, became the powerful Secretary of State in 1660 and Duke of Lauderdale in 1672 and must be considered potentially one of Barlow's most useful patrons. Barlow dedicated a set of bird prints to his nephew Richard Maitland sometime between 1682 and 1691.

Of the other extant Barlow paintings the one at the Tate Gallery, unsigned and undated [1689?] (fig. 1), might be mentioned because of its accessibility. A pair of honey buzzards, arrogant in their cruel beauty, rest on the dead branch of a tree. The male looks up at a passing bird. The female looks down at three new-born owlets, improbably exposed on a flat rock. A parent owl ineffectually spreads its wings to shield them. The wild mountains suggest Scotland, but as in other

1) BARLOW, *Honey buzzards and owlets*, 1060 × 1371 mm.

Barlow paintings the scene serves only as a dark backdrop. Essentially he is preserving an exact likeness of two fresh-killed or stuffed honey buzzards (their
claws do not curl round the branch). Then he borrows (we hope) three owlets not
only to do their portraits but, as if in a fable illustration, to show the buzzards in a
revealing relationship at the moment before what would be over-explicit action.
In the J. Pierpont Morgan collection is a drawing, signed and dated 1689, of a
vulture bending down to the same three owlets. It was engraved by Francis Place
for *Divers Species of Birds*.

It misses the point to look on Barlow's paintings as one would those of Turner,
Cézanne, or even Chardin. Barlow never uses his subjects as an exercise in creating beauty, in solving technical problems, or even in selective realism. His paint-
ings are documentaries. He is imbued with the spirit of the age, or at least of the
Royal Society. The Dr. Wilkins who in 1656 took Evelyn to see the 'famous
Paynter of fowle Beastes & Birds' and who presumably was either Barlow's
friend or well acquainted with him, was Dr. John Wilkins (1614–1672). Under
Charles I he had become Warden of Wadham College, Oxford (1648); in 1656 he
married the sister of Oliver Cromwell, who made him Master of Trinity College,
Cambridge. After 1660 he was the vicar of St. Lawrence Jewry in London and
ultimately Bishop of Chester. Wilkins was a moving spirit in the small group who
as early as 1645 met to discuss what in that exciting morning of science they
broadly considered scientific matters, who continued to do so at Oxford during
the Civil War, and who in 1662 received from Charles II a charter as the Royal
Society, with Wilkins as the first chairman and Evelyn a charter member. Wilkins,
who was especially interested in mathematics, astronomy, and mechanics (he invented a drogue), was influential in introducing experimental methods at Oxford
and Cambridge. The interests of the Society easily embraced Barlow's drawings
and paintings: Evelyn and Prince Rupert showed active curiosity about graphic
processes. Indeed the injunction of the Society that its members observe a 'close,
naked, natural way of speaking, positive expressions, clear senses, a native easi-
ness' comes close to describing Barlow's style. And his aim was consonant with
that of the Society – to record accurately and completely the facts about some
aspect of the physical world, specifically the wild and domestic creatures that
played so large a part in the economy, recreation, and consciousness of English
society.

Barlow apparently painted few portraits besides the one of General Monk. A
full-length boy and his groom belongs to the Tyrwhitt-Drake collection, and one
of the third Viscount Irwin loading the muzzle of a musket while his dog retrieves
the pheasant he has just shot seems to be by Barlow though unsigned. It is at
Temple Newsam House, Leeds (Waterhouse, pl. 69).

His Drawings

A surprising number of Barlow's drawings are extant, but they are scattered and many remain uncertainly identified. Fortunately, the exceptional collection at the British Museum has been thoroughly catalogued by Croft-Murray and Hulton (here abbreviated C-M&H) with numerous reproductions. Other drawings are reproduced in books listed in the Bibliography. A goodly number are in the Witt Collection at the Courtauld Institute Gallery (Woburn Square), the Ashmolean Museum, the Henry E. Huntington Collection, and other collections, and others must be lying unidentified elsewhere. Many reproductions of Barlow's work and some original prints are also in the Witt archives at the Courtauld Institute (Portman Square).

Barlow usually drew in brown ink with a pen – *i.e.*, a quill. Sometimes he used a pencil or 'plumbago', plain graphite. Then he applied a grey wash – ink thinned with water – to indicate form and shadows. His drawings are almost always carefully and rather heavily outlined and finished. They are generally meant to be transferred to a copper plate for facsimile reproduction, often by another hand, and they seem meant to be preserved, possibly for gift or sale or safeguard against disaster to the plate, as well as for pleasure. A few of those that have been etched or engraved show hardly discernible outlining with a pointed instrument and traces of black lead or red chalk (bolus) on the back as evidence of transfer. According to Faithorne's *Art of Graveing and Etching* (1662), the transfer was made easier by first giving the plate a thin coating of wax. The drawing could be protected by blacking the back of a thin sheet of paper and inserting it, like carbon paper, between the drawing and the plate. Similar treatises recommend other transfer methods.

For our purpose Barlow's drawings may be put into four groups: birds and animals, book illustrations, miscellaneous, and contemporary affairs.

Birds and animals, wild and domestic, were so intimate and important a part of English life before the Industrial Revolution that they appear constantly in drawings from the earliest days of English art. But Barlow contributes three fresh emphases: accuracy of recording based on prolonged study of living and dead models, in accordance with the awakening scientific spirit of the age; an understanding of wild creatures' habits and their relation to their environment; and a positive delight in their forms, motion, and personalities. His drawings are the best vehicle of this complex awareness. Much of the feeling – sometimes all – is lost in the prints and illustrations made from his drawings.

Two drawings show different aspects of his approach. A herd of deer at the Ashmolean (fig. 2) shows his almost photographic veracity, and the soft effects

2) BARLOW, *Animals in a landscape*, 243 × 328 mm.

3) BARLOW, *Rooster and turkey fighting*, 185 × 296 mm.

prove that his heavy outline in other drawings may be only an aid in transfer to a plate or sometimes the result of the transfer. As Woodward says (*Tudor & Stuart Drawings*, p. 25), 'Birds and beasts of the English countryside had been popular subjects for the borders of medieval manuscripts, but Barlow was the first to restore them to their true setting of fields, trees, and ponds.' The fight between a rooster and a turkey from the Courtauld Institute Gallery (fig. 3) reveals Barlow's quiet passion for precise observation, from the posture of the combatants to the look of the chicks and the construction of the farm gate. In his drawings Barlow also reveals best his astonishing ability to recreate creatures in movements seen only for the blink of an eye or not at all.

Although for example he made a trip to Scotland where he saw and recorded an eagle and cat in aerial combat, Barlow utilised the work of predecessors for some animals and birds from distant places. (Versions of the rhinoceros by many artists go back to Dürer's famous drawing, and many another creature's form and features can be traced back to one of the works of Conrad von Gesner.) But strange animals were brought to England from very early times. According to Bennett's *The Tower Menagerie* (1829) Henry III had three leopards at Woodstock, in 1252 a white bear kept in the Tower of London was taken to fish and wash in the Thames, in 1255 quarters for an elephant had to be built in the Tower, and in 1657 Barlow could have observed six lions there. Unusual birds and animals were also exhibited in taverns. An indefatigable sketcher from life, Barlow did not lack for models, some of which were stuffed or recently dead.

We shall not look at Barlow's drawings for book illustrations until we come to the books. At the Ashmolean Museum, however, are six pen-and-wash drawings (average 66 × 70 mm.) for illustrations to Ovid's *Metamorphoses*. They have been ascribed to Barlow tentatively, but they seem to be some of the original drawings by F. Chauveau for a Paris edition (1676). Thirteen drawings (*c.* 35 × 44 mm.) which seem intended for illustrations to a book about a war, or conceivably for a deck of playing cards, which are at the National Gallery of Scotland, have also been ascribed to Barlow. On the basis of comparison with his playing-card drawings in the British Museum, this ascription seems plausible. The same boldly accented style is present in both, and the horses seem closely similar. Mr. Paul Hulton of the British Museum, however, has kindly examined the originals in Edinburgh and does not think that they are by Barlow. Certainly the battle scenes, including a woman leader and what seem fleur-de-lys and double-headed-eagle standards, look continental.

In the miscellaneous group of drawings is Barlow's earliest surviving dated work, his carefully composed and detailed 'David Slaying the Lion' (206 × 295 mm.) (C-M&H, pl. 49), signed with the young artist's self-conscious 'Francis Barlow/inventer/1648'. An expressionless David raises a scimitar while he restrains a lion with Mongolian eyes by pulling its head around by the whiskers. A lamb lies passively as in a Christmas tableau. A shepherd's crook makes a base for a contrived isosceles triangle. Nine undated heads on one sheet (C-M&H, pl. 50) drawn about the same time seem studies of family or friends. From the beginning Barlow is a conscientious realist.

Three of the drawings in the Henry E. Huntington Collection, reproduced by Wark, can be dated approximately. They reveal Barlow doing what came to hand through the years in a bitterly divided society. The first is not signed but seems correctly assigned to Barlow. It is a large full-length portrait (567 × 424 mm.) of Oliver Cromwell in armour surrounded by symbolic objects. It was engraved by William Faithorne under the title 'The Embleme of England's Distraction' (1658) as a tribute to the Protector the year of his death. A signed drawing of two heralds, the Rougecroix Pursuivant and Rougedragon, is for a long engraving celebrating the coronation of the Duke of York as James II (1685). Then Barlow inscribed 'F Barlow del. No. 6' on a decorative panel with the arms of William III on a proscenium arch above a public building (not Kensington Palace) in the background, a fountain, and an ape, and hawk sitting on a balustrade. It clearly was part of a series to be engraved, doubtless with text, probably in connection with William of Orange becoming king in 1688.

An unsigned sketch (78 × 228 mm.), certainly by Barlow, at the British Museum has been cut out but seems intended to go below an engraved or etched portrait of Peter I of Russia (1672–1725). 'Peter Alexeewitz the Great Czar of Moscow' is lightly roughed in on both sides of Peter's coat of arms on a fox skin attached to two hooks with the fox's head preserved at the top, the severed forepaws dangling from the hooks and the hind paws lying horizontal. Perhaps the last of Barlow's drawings that can be dated, in itself the sketch is insignificant. The tall young ruler came to England in January 1697/8 as a guest of William III. He stayed in Norfolk Street, except in February and March when he was learning shipbuilding by working with his hands at Deptford. While he was there, the King hired Sayes Court, John Evelyn's country home, for him. (Wren later estimated the damage at £150.) Possibly Barlow's sketch was engraved to go below an engraved copy of Kneller's portrait of Peter, which William III commissioned to commemorate Peter's visit to Kensington Palace and which now hangs there. Presumably Barlow drew the portrait or whatever was on the rest of the design, but it is improbable that he etched the plate himself. It is enough to know that he was engaged in such up-to-the-minute work when he was over seventy.

Social Commentary

That brings us to the fourth group, those drawings with contemporary social relevance. It is natural to wonder what difference the shocks of political change made in Barlow's career. He seems to have done better during the Interregnum than one would have imagined an artist would do, but the evidence is sketchy. We have mentioned the drawing of Cromwell for 'The Embleme of England's Distraction' (1658). With the Restoration of the monarchy in 1660 and the growth of England as a mercantile power, we should expect Barlow's fortunes to improve. His ownership of 'The Golden Eagle' and his turning publisher of his folio Aesop confirm this expectation. But the Plague and the Fire were serious setbacks. And not only did Charles II and his exilic companions encourage foreign artists and engravers at the expense of their own countrymen. They did little to encourage book illustration in the way they did portrait painting, architecture, decoration, and drama.

It is therefore understandable, if at first surprising, to see the attention Barlow gave to contemporary events, both as a reporter and as a social satirist. In fact, Barlow adds another first to his record – the first known native artist of ability to work seriously in reportage and what we now call political cartooning (as distinct from simple caricature). Hollar anticipated Barlow both as reporter and propagandist by many years, but he was neither English-born nor up to his usual level in this mode. The 'Procession of the Knights of the Garter' (1576) by Gheeraerts was even earlier. Woodcuts and engravings had long decorated informational, propagandistic, and satirical broadsides, and a large number of the illustrations in Foxe's *Actes and Monuments* and Holinshed's *Chronicles* of a century before are really a superior form of graphic journalism, and some are essentially political cartoons. But Barlow seems the first identifiable English artist of any distinction to have dealt with contemporary affairs before Hogarth.

4) BARLOW, *Drawing for Popish Plot playing cards*, 78 × 52 mm.

What makes Barlow's social commentary the more remarkable is that his topical drawings were reproduced not only as prints but also as playing cards and ceramic tiles. About 1680 he made drawings (average: 66, 78 × 52 mm.) for two packs of anti-Jesuit, anti-Rome playing cards, one set in the British Museum recording incidents and alleged incidents in the infamous Titus Oates 'Popish

Plot' (1678) (fig. 4) and the other the 'Meal Tub Plot' (1680) by which some Roman Catholics misguidedly tried to retaliate. Before that he may have made a set for a Rump Parliament pack. These are all small rapidly drawn scenes which show Barlow as a master of journalistic and propagandistic directness. The legends written below the drawings by Barlow make it seem probable that he conceived the series himself. These drawings, though designed for playing cards, are in effect illustrations of scenes, whether actual or fabricated, that Barlow imagined. As we have suggested, he may have been in the pay of William Cavendish, later the Earl of Devonshire.

In his *Descriptive Catalogue of the Engraved Works of William Faithorne* (1888) L. Fagan incorrectly listed a complete deck of cards as engraved by Faithorne after Barlow's 'Popish Plot' designs. In *English Delftware Tiles* (1973) A. Ray reproduces a set of nine tiles from the Schreiber Collection at the Victoria and Albert Museum. They are listed (no. 823) in the catalogue of that collection (1885) as made at Lambeth. While some designs for tiles were apparently borrowed from engraved playing cards, these nine circular designs are brush-drawn copies of Barlow's 'Popish Plot' drawings. They are so much in Barlow's style that they seem probably to have been drawn by him. C. E. Hargrave in *A History of Playing Cards* (1966) quotes a notice in the *Public Advertiser* of 17 December 1759 for a set of cards with designs from 'Aesop's Fables exactly copied after Barlow, with fables and morals in verse' for sale by I. Kirk, and she adds, 'There is no other known example of these little cards.' It is significant that Barlow's name was well enough known in 1759 to be used in this way. There are also ceramic tiles with designs taken from Elisha Kirkall's illustrations for Samuel Croxall's *Fables of Aesop and Others* (1722). Many of these are derived from Barlow's designs.

Political Cartoons

Three exceptional political cartoons by Barlow establish his place as the first Englishman to apply the hand of a master to this lowly but influential genre. Two are etchings and one is a drawing. In view of the nature of these ephemerae, undoubtedly other examples have totally disappeared, received no public notice, not been identified, or been attributed to other artists.

The first, a satirical etching in the British Museum, signed 'R Gaywood fecit' [1670?], was certainly drawn by Barlow (fig. 5). According to the explanation for no. 1034 in the British Museum catalogue, *Political and Personal Satires,* the cow represents Holland with the King of Spain on her back and an unidentified prince enjoying her milk, while Charles II, the King of Denmark, the Bishop of Munster, and Louis XIV (or the Duke of York) feed and hold her. The central

5) BARLOW, *Holland satirically depicted as a cow*, 148 × 219 mm.

R. Gaywood fecit

figure of the cow has all the naturalness of a Barlow animal, something never attained, if ever attempted, by Gaywood. The human figures resemble those in frontispieces designed by Barlow and etched by Gaywood. In spite of its shape and broadside character, this etching is said to be a frontispiece, which together with a nine-stanza explanatory poem, has been detached from an unidentified book.

Another rough satire against the Dutch from the British Museum (fig. 6) is an unsigned, undated etching offered for sale by Edward Powell and George Farthing [c. 1673]. Powell shared in selling Barlow's *Aesop's Fables* (1666). The Dutch are ridiculed as spawn of the Devil and are shown inside and issuing from a large cut-out egg, on top of which the horrible Devil himself crouches. As he seizes one of the men from around a table inside, he says, 'What thou may'st be, as yet I cannott tell/But Butterbox [a Dutchman] is the worst food in Hell'. The three quatrains at the top of the broadside and the eleven other rude rimes in the comic-strip ribbons are fairly general propagandist attacks on the Dutch. No. 1045 of the catalogue, *Political and Personal Satires*, gives the text with explanations.

The example at the British Museum has been incorrectly assigned to Gaywood. Only Barlow could have drawn the devils, small animals, and even the worms with such gusto and authority. Even more conclusive, the Dutchman falling out of the egg (LC) shows more than a casual likeness to the terrified small boy in Barlow's illustration of 'The Countryman and the Snake' (fig. 91). In spite of the coarseness of some of the satire, Barlow draws the Dutch without degrading them, including the one amusingly riding a fish. He complains: 'Myne Broders hear me, I am come to tell,/We must goe seek another place to dwell,/Our Fleet's disabled, and our Toadstool Throne/Is sinking now, for we are left alone.' He resembles somewhat the jousters on their unlikely mounts in Cleyn and Barlow's illustrations for the Homeric fable of 'The Battle of the Mice and Frogs'.

The third political cartoon by Barlow is at the Ashmolean Museum. It is a drawing of two armed apes, one mounted on a bear confronting the other on a boar, each with an ape attendant on foot, the two sides exchanging insults across a stream (fig. 7). It is signed by Barlow and dated 1679 (not 1699 as at first appears) and is all ready for engraving as a large broadside, though it seems not to have been engraved. According to one plausible reading, the figure on the bear may stand for Emperor Leopold I (the Holy Roman Empire), and the figure on the boar certainly represents King Louis XIV (France) – the Gallic cock and three shuttlecocks in place of fleurs-de-lys settle that. The foot-soldier under the insignia of the ass on the left may be Charles V, the Duke of Lorraine, and the one on the right King Charles II (England). At this time Charles II was in the pay of Louis, though not very useful to him as it turned out. The horn-blowing owl

6) BARLOW, *Dutchmen hatched by the Devil*, 255 × 328 mm.

with the standard of crossed artichokes (for St. Peter's crossed keys) seems meant to represent the Papacy on the side of the Emperor (though Louis was Catholic, he and the Pope were at odds). The snipe blowing the horn under the insignia of three mushrooms (for three crowns) seems to symbolize King Charles XI of Sweden, at the time on the side of France.

In modern spelling the inscriptions and doggerel speeches written hastily for the engraver apparently by Barlow himself (his book on hawking, hunting, and fishing is in similar couplets) are as follows (L to R):

> *Major Lick Trencher* [Duke of Lorraine?]: We walk but slow ... but we be sure/And these affronts no longer shall endure.

> [*Emperor Leopold I?*]: Come, Monsieur good Sir Huft [Captain Huff, a bragging soldier], I shall so pault [beat] your brain/I'll make you spew my apple up again./Your shabroon [ragamuffin] rout shall soon my country fly/Like shuttlecocks I'll make them mount the sky.

> [*King Louis XIV*]: Be gone (?) Gaston (?), you are the son of a whore and know/I'll have your country where the apple grow[s]./No matter whether the war be false or right,/'Tis for my glory that I now do fight.

> *Captain Suck Plume* [King Charles II?]: Sa sah along [ça ça allonge, cry to begin a duel]! Ten thousand pug (?) [apes (?)] me slay/Then turn my arse and bravely run away.

According to the tentative explanation advanced above, the 'apple' that is the cause of this confrontation would be Lorraine. The river would then be the Meuse. In his restless acquiring and disencumbering himself of real estate, Louis had taken Lorraine from the Empire; then in the Treaty of 26 February 1679 he had ceded it back to the Duke of Lorraine but had continued to keep troops there. There may be a better explanation than this: Louis snatched many apples. In this last quarter of the century patronage had shifted to the politicians. Like the playing cards these two cartoons may have been made to please or even at the behest of William Cavendish. In 1677 Cavendish was active in having the British troops withdrawn from the service of the French.

If the interpretation of the apes jousting given above is not correct, the correct interpretation will be much the same. We are concerned with what it reveals about Francis Barlow. Barlow's drawing is worlds away from the laboured allegories and brutal attacks common in the broadsides of the day, of which his devil and egg cartoon is unfortunately typical despite its superior draughtsmanship. This joust satire does not go beyond even-handed good-natured ridicule of foreigners. The low-level dialogue is the ritualistic trading of insults by school-

7) BARLOW, *Drawing for a political cartoon satirizing Louis XIV and others*, 214 × 314 mm.

boys – and Barlow never imagined his beasts crossing that brook. His heart is in drawing them – his bear, boar, apes, owl, and snipe, all lovingly articulated from eyes to feet, together with their trappings, beribboned costumes, baroque horns, and homicidal gear. It is natural that when he comes to draw a political cartoon, Barlow should translate nations and their synonymous leaders into animals and birds, but these he cannot make appear bestial. Political cartoons are but fables, and Barlow uses the traditional Aesopic confrontation – more exactly, his own illustration for the battle of the mice and frogs – to serve a satirical purpose. In so doing he creates not only a masterpiece among English topical drawings but a model of the humorous, realistic, well-drawn political cartoon that will come to be the pride of English journalism a century and a half later.

A vigorous etching at the British Museum, St. George slaying the dragon, fits in here (fig. 8). It is dedicated to Sir Edward Bish (Bysshe). Although it is not a political cartoon, the subject has many times been given topical applications. In fact, Barlow's inspiration seems to have been Gheeraerts' 'William of Orange as St. George'. But Barlow executes the familiar motif in his own manner. The print is one of his most satisfactory etchings, one in which controlled biting achieves tonal effects that soften his usual linear style.

The print not only has Barlow's initials on a stone in the lower right corner; he puts his name to the Latin dedication to Sir Edward Bysshe (*c.* 1616–1679). The first state was sold by Arthur Tooker 'against Salisbury hous'. By the second state – the one reproduced here – Tooker had in 1669 moved to Ivy Bridge. Bysshe was knighted in 1661. Barlow probably etched the print nearer to 1661 than to 1669 because Bysshe would have seemed a more promising patron then. During the Interregnum he had been a member of Parliament, had prospered as Garter king of arms and Clarenceux, and had encouraged learned men. In 1660 he was deprived of his heraldic offices, but in 1661 was restored to favour and knighted for preserving the library of the College of Arms during the Civil War. But after the Restoration he was much in debt and dishonestly sold grants of arms. After 1702 the St. George appeared in an altered third state with a bored-looking Britannia taking the place of the maiden and with a new dedication to Prince George, the consort of Queen Anne, engraved in place of the original one. Barlow's initials were shaded over and his name removed from the dedication.

*   *   *   *   *

Francis Barlow lived to what in the seventeenth century was the extremely advanced age of seventy-eight or so, perhaps because his love of sports and wild creatures made him spend much of his time outdoors. He was active until 1703,

8) BARLOW, *St. George slaying the dragon*, 274 × 213 mm.

the year before his death. We should like to know more about his personal life. He was prominent enough in his day to be noticed; probably what has been handed down and what can be inferred are substantially true. It would be more useful to know more about the practical details of his work as artist, illustrator, and publisher. More light will certainly be shed on his professional career when as many as possible of his extant drawings, prints, and paintings have been located and recorded in a catalogue raisonné, though many must be already lost or will remain undetected. But there seems no reason to doubt that we have access to all of Barlow's significant illustrated books. In a list of 'Plates of Mr. Gaywood's Etching, invented by Mr. Barlow and others' advertised by the print dealer Arthur Tooker in 1675 is included 'A book of 27 Leaves, of several Stories of the beginning of the Bible'. If extant, this could prove to be by Barlow.

We can now go on to examine his work as a book illustrator and that of the three artists linked with him.

CHAPTER II

Book Illustration In England
Before 1700

To UNDERSTAND how it happens that no native-born illustrator came before
Barlow or arose during his lifetime, a short review of book illustration in
England before 1700 is necessary. In fact, the first known artist to illustrate a
printed book in England is Marcus Gheeraerts the elder, and the book is dated
1568. Until then the account of English illustrated books must be told by means
of the printers who printed and sold them. And yet the first half-century of printing in England was, if not a golden age for the illustrated book, certainly one of
abundance. About 900 illustrated books printed before 1535 survive; they contain about 2700 woodcuts. Two-thirds of these books were printed by the three
leading printer-publishers of the first generation.

Caxton, De Worde, Pynson, and other Early Printers

William Caxton (1422?–1491) did not issue an illustrated book for five years after
he set up the first English printing press outside the Chapter House of
Westminster Abbey in 1476. Then he introduced four hundred woodcuts into a
score of books. They were either imported used blocks or clumsy copies of continental illustrations. There were in England neither the artists to draw original
designs nor the skilled craftsmen to cut blocks properly. Nevertheless, the
imported blocks, though sometimes badly worn, were members of traditional
religious series that admirably served their didactic purpose, and the copied
blocks presented the same designs as their continental originals. Their rough
cutting could not have offended readers who were looking at the miracle of printing for the first time, any more than the imperfections of Edison's wax cylinders
disturbed anyone in rural America on first hearing Caruso's voice.

The first illustrated book printed in England by Caxton is *The Myrroure of the
World* (1481) with several miserable woodcuts, obviously the first and last efforts
of a workman in the shop. Thereafter Caxton either bought used woodcut blocks
from the Continent or had a second man, unskilled but not so inept as the first,

make traced copies of continental series. Caxton's most important illustrated books, two religious and two non-religious, are Jacobus de Voragine's *Legenda aurea* (after 20 Nov. 1483) (designs copied), Bonaventura's *Speculum vitae Christi* (second-hand blocks), *Fables of Esope* (1484) (copies), and Chaucer's *Canterbury Tales* (1484?) [designs based on a lost manuscript].

Wynkyn de Worde (d. 1534) of Alsace, Caxton's assistant and successor in 1491, used Caxton's blocks in reprints of Caxton's books and in other books for which they were not designed, and he followed his master's example by buying and copying continental series. Since Caxton's woodcuts for *The Canterbury Tales* are merely cuts of the pilgrims and not illustrations of their stories, the bizarre woodcuts in De Worde's edition of Malory's *Morte d'Arthur* (1498) (fig. 9) are the first original interpretive illustrations of a major work of English literature in a printed book. De Worde brought out about fifty illustrated secular works, including the *Boke of Hawkynge* (fig. 10), *Mandeville's Travels*, Brant's *Ship of Fools, Reynard the Fox*, and Chaucer's *Troilus and Criseyde*. He must especially be remembered for a significant number of modest octavos of popular

9) ANON, from Malory: *Morte d'Arthur* (Wynkyn de Worde 1498), 95 × 122 mm.

romances like *Valentine and Orson Oliver of Castile, Four Sons of Aymon, King Ponthus, King Richard Cuer du Lyon Elias Knight of the Swan, Bevis of Hampton*, and *Huon of Bordeaux*. In spite of the fact that his illustrations are virtually all traced copies of French originals, he is an important force in popularizing the illustrated book in England.

Although Richard Pynson (d. 1530), a Norman, specialized in legal and other practical works, he had the best taste in typography (he introduced Roman type) and illustrations of all the early printers. He imported and copied excellent French relief metal and woodcut blocks belonging to Dupré, Pigouchet, Vérard, and other leading printers of France. His chief copyist-cutter was the best to practise in England for several decades, but he did no original work. In addition to some impressive religious books, Pynson issued relatively few popular works, the most important being Aesop's *Fables*, Boccaccio's *Fall of Princes*, Chaucer's major poems, *Reynard the Fox, Bevis of Hampton*, Brant's *Ship of Fools* (fig. 11), *The Destruction of Jerusalem*, and *The History of Troy*. Sometimes early illustration presents puzzles. Pynson used Caxton's woodcuts for an edition of Aesop's *Fables* in

The fourth boke.

10) ANON, from *The Boke of Hawkynge* (Wynkyn de Worde 1496), 92 × 109 mm.

11) ANON, from Brant: *Ship of Fools* (Richard Pynson 1509), 112 × 81 mm.

1497, and then a few years later printed another edition with improved copies of the same blocks. Perhaps he shared the earlier edition with De Worde, who presumably owned the blocks, as in 1507 they collaborated on a *Boke Named the Royall* and a *Legenda aurea*. Usually, however, Pynson and De Worde were rivals. In 1507 they published competing editions of Gringore's *Castle of Labour* and in 1509 Brant's *Ship of Fools* with virtually identical illustrations copied from the original continental series.

Julyan Notary, Peter Treveris, and the other dozen or so printers in the first third of the century brought out a fair number of illustrated books, some of respectable quality and interest but not of originality. Many of the wood-blocks owned by Caxton, De Worde, and Pynson passed to other printers and are to be found, worn and wormholed, in books throughout the sixteenth century. Indeed, after the enthusiasm for filling popular books with illustrations had begun to diminish sharply about 1520, book illustration in England was in a depressed state for many years. A glorious day might have dawned when Hans Holbein, one of the great book illustrators, came to work in England in 1532, but he was kept busy painting portraits and died in the plague of 1543 before he got round to illustrating a single English book or training one English illustrator. Holbein did design a splendid title-page border used for the first complete Bible in English (1535), translated by the Protestant scholars Tyndale and Coverdale, but it was printed in Germany. The seventy superb small woodcuts in this first English Bible are by Hans Sebald Beham and had appeared the year before in a Catholic Bible printed in Mainz. The illustrations in other famous Tudor Bibles – the 'Matthew Bible' (1537), Cranmer's 'Great Bible' (1539), and the 'Bishops' Bible' (1568) – have similar histories.

Burin engraving on metal was introduced to England in 1540 in poor anonymous copies of eighteen diagrams in a German book of midwifery. Then in 1545 Thomas Geminus engraved forty pages of anatomical figures for a book on anatomy. They are traced copies of the fine woodcuts in Vesalius' two folios first printed in Basle in 1543. According to Auerbach, Geminus was a Belgian named Gemyny (and Lambrit) from Lixhe near Liége, who died in Canterbury in 1562. Intaglio engraving on metal, however, was not used for interpretive illustration in England for fifty years.

John Heywood's *The Spider and the Flies* (John Powell, 1556) is one of the few interesting illustrated books published during the middle decades of the century. It contains a novel full-length portrait of Heywood and forty-seven cleanly drawn and cut designs of the poet, the flies, spiders, a butterfly, and a maid (Queen Mary), who take part in this Catholic allegory (fig. 12). Although repetition of each of the blocks spoils their effect, *The Spider and the Flies* is notable both for the clean cutting of the woodcuts and for their being freshly made for the text they illustrate.

John Day and Henry Bynneman

The most significant figure in the history of English book illustration in the second half of the sixteenth century is the innovative printer John Day (1522–1684). Apart from advancing the Protestant cause and the state of typography, he issued a number of books with fresh illustrations. They include Cuningham's *Cosmographical Glasse* (1559), Foxe's *Actes and Monuments* (1563, 1570), Van der

12) ANON, from Heywood: *The Spider and the Flies*, 112 × 92 mm.

Noot's *Theatre* (1568), Bateman's *A Christall Glasse* (1569), North's *The Morall Philosophie of Doni* (1570), Grosseteste's *Testaments of the twelve Patriarches* (1575), and Derrick's *Image of Irelande* (1581).

The *Cosmographical Glasse* is the first book printed in England with signed illustrations. The evidence seems to indicate that IB was the designer, and ID was the woodcutter. The possibility that IB was John Bettes, a miniaturist, seems slight.

John Foxe's *Actes and Monuments*, popularly known as *The Book of Martyrs*, although intended mainly as a history of Protestantism in England, was avidly perused by all classes of Britons for three centuries. It is perhaps the most conspicuous example of an English book in which the illustrations have had as vivid and lasting an impact on readers as the author's own words. In the enlarged second edition of 1570 there are a hundred and four woodcuts of great graphic power, including sixty-five large ones, forty-seven from the first edition. The most famous are those of terrible martyrdoms (fig. 13), but others represent

13) ANON, from Foxe: *Actes and Monuments* (1583), 124 × 174 mm.

14) ANON, from *Actes and Monuments*, 180 × 169 mm.

fascinating scenes often from contemporary history (fig. 14). The blocks were designed by perhaps two artists of considerable competence and cut by at least two able craftsmen.

Van der Noot's *Theatre* and Bateman's *A Christall Glasse* will be discussed with the work of Marcus Gheeraerts in Chapter III.

The forty-nine woodcuts (*c.* 70 × 80 mm.) for Sir Thomas North's translation from the Italian of *The morall philosophie of Doni*, fables and tales going back to Bidpai, are about the earliest illustrations in an English book that are consciously and successfully diverting. They were cut for Day's edition, but they probably have Italian forbears. The same hand seems to have made thirteen fresh blocks for *Testaments of the twelve Patriarches, the Sonnes of Jacob*. The title-page block of the dying Jacob and his twelve sons is signed RB. He presumably cut all the blocks and those for *The morall philosophie of Doni*. The *Twelve Patriarches* woodcuts, followed by descriptive verse preceding the advice of the sons to their children are, like Gheeraerts' *Theatre* illustrations, predecessors of the emblem books in England.

The last of John Day's books on our list, John Derricke's *The Image of Irelande* (1581), deserves a place of honour in the history of English book illustration. It is a verse celebration of the subjugation of the Irish 'wood kerns' by Sir Henry Sidney, Philip's father, in 1575. Six of the twelve large illustrations of the campaign are probably the finest woodcuts to be made especially for an English book, both in the beauty and dignity of their complex designs and in the skill of their cutting (fig. 15). Four of the blocks are signed FD and two ID, presumably the initials of the cutters. The designs must be original, but the artist may have been influenced by the similar illustrations of armies in the field in Tortorel and Perrissin's *Quarante tableaux ou histoires diuerses qui sont memorables touchant les guerres, massacres, & troubles aduenus en France en ses dernières années* (1570).

Besides *A Christall Glasse* printed by Day, the prolific Stephen Bateman was the author of illustrated editions of *The Trauayled Pylgrime* (Henry Denham, 1569), *The New Arival of the three Gracis into Anglia* (Thomas East, [1580?]), and *The Doom Warning* (Ralph Newbery 'under assignment to Henry Bynneman', 1581). Since each of Bateman's four books has a different printer, we may imagine that he is our first instance of an author, like Dickens and Shaw, with positive ideas about the illustrating of his works. Although the twenty woodcuts for *The Trauayled Pylgrime* are not lively, they are original efforts to interpret the author's journey through time. He appears in each illustration with other figures and symbols, and each has an interpretation printed with it, another anticipation of emblem books. Bateman's *The New Arival of the three Gracis, into Anglia* contains three appropriate woodcuts.

15) ANON, from Derricke: *The Image of Irelande*, 168 × 301 mm.

Next to John Day, Henry Bynneman (d. 1583) is the most enterprising printer of illustrated books in the second half of the sixteenth century. The two woodcuts in George Turbervile's *Booke of Faulconrie or Hawking* (1575) and the four in the anonymous companion work of the same date, *The Noble Arte of Venerie or Hunting*, are fascinating for their views of Queen Elizabeth and her courtiers in contemporary costumes and the detailed post-De Worde and pre-Barlow views of hawking and hunting (fig. 16). Again, these must be illustrations made specifically for this text. Both drawing and cutting are excellent – and, alas, of course, anonymous.

Bynneman's same hand seems to have anticipated Elisha Kirkall in rediscovering the art of engraving in relief on metal in a cut of a hermit and a mounted noble in Elizabethan costume for *The Mirror of Man's Life, Englisshed by H.K.* (1576). Bynneman's most important illustrated book is Holinshed's *Chronicles of England, Scotlande, and Irelande* (1577), which he printed for John Harrison. Because there is reason to believe that Gheeraerts was the chief illustrator, it will be discussed in Chapter III.

16) ANON, from *The Noble Arte of Venerie*, 99 × 112 mm.

The End of the Sixteenth Century

In Edmund Spenser's *Shepheardes Calendar* (Hugh Singleton, 1579) a dozen poorly cut oblong woodcuts (59 × 102 mm.) picture the pastoral events for the twelve months. Only the importance of the work in the development of English literature makes it desirable to note the illustrations in passing. Spenser receives even less reverence in the first edition of *The Faerie Queene* (1590). It has only one illustration, a casual woodcut of St. George slaying the dragon. (Shakespeare had to wait until 1709 for his first illustrated edition.) The printer Henry Denham secured the services of a competent hand for Thomas Bentley's *Monument of Matrones* (1582). He engraved on metal in relief three title-page borders and an oval illustration of the Last Judgment.

Towards the end of the sixteenth century none of the few noteworthy illustrated books can be said to contain original English designs. The hundreds of woodcuts of plants in the *Niewe Herball* (1578) were originally drawn by Pieter van der Borcht for Christopher Plantin, and the many hundreds in the Gerard *Herball* (1597, 1633) appeared first in Frankfurt and Antwerp. The fifteen woodcuts in *The Strife of Loue in a Dream* (1592), a partial translation of Colonna's *Hypnerotomachia Poliphili*, are only fair copies of the famous set in the Aldus edition (Venice, 1499).

The first edition of Broughton's *A Concent of Scripture* [1590?] has bound in at the end five anti-Catholic emblematic plates, said by Hind to be by the Ghent map-maker Jocodus Hondius, a visitor for ten years. They apparently are the first interpretive illustrations in a book printed in England to be burin engraved on metal. The best known engraved illustrations in an English book before 1700 are the forty-six large plates in Harington's translation of Ariosto's *Orlando Furioso* (1591) (fig. 17). They are, however, facsimile copies of Porro's engravings in a Venetian edition of 1584, which in turn go back ultimately to the splendid woodcuts in the Valgrisi edition (Venice, 1556). These large designs represent the chief events in each canto in the medieval manner – that is, with the characters diminishing in size as they are shown in receding planes in several incidents.

In some introductory remarks Harington gives us the first critical comment on book illustrating by an Englishman. Illustrations are useful, he announces, because after you have read a book, you can read it again in pictures. Even less illuminating are his dicta that perspective is the 'chief art in a picture' and that engravings on 'brass' [copper] are superior to woodcuts because 'the more cost the more worship'. The illustrations in Harington's *Orlando Furioso* and his opinions mark the rise in popularity of intaglio metal engraving in books printed in England and the banishment of woodcuts to popular prints. This shift in taste had taken place on the Continent years before.

17) ANON, after Porro, from Ariosto: *Orlando Furioso*, trans. Harrington, 192 × 134 mm.

The Seventeenth Century

In fact, however, throughout the seventeenth century in England burin engraving is mainly used for portrait frontispieces, ornamental title-pages, and maps, and relatively rarely for interpretive illustration. Besides the Bible and four classics to be discussed in Chapter IV, only a few books printed in England before 1700 contain engraved illustrations at all comparable to the *Orlando Furioso* series. As already indicated, the etchers Cleyn, Hollar, and Barlow dominate the century. Since their books are the business of the following chapters, they will not be discussed in this one. Three considerations have some bearing on the decline of interpretive illustration in the seventeenth century. We have noted that intaglio plates – metal engravings and etchings – are expensive and have to be printed separately from type. The long struggle between the Crown and Parliament and the Puritan disapproval of light entertainment discouraged the printing of *belles-lettres* during the mid-years. And then plays and lyric poetry were the fashionable forms of literature during the Elizabethan and Jacobean years and the Restoration, and they have never been much illustrated. The illustrated novel, successor to De Worde and Pynson's romances, did not appear until the eighteenth century.

Emblem Books

Emblem books, tremendously popular on the Continent during the sixteenth century, came belatedly to England. In an emblem book the brief text and the picture, or device, are mutually descriptive. Therefore, since English poets gave the texts a fresh religious complexion, new energy might have been breathed into the illustrations. It was not. Geffrey Whitney's *A Choice of Emblemes*, generally considered the first emblem book in English, was printed at Leiden in 1586 and illustrated with old woodcuts from Christopher Plantin's various series. *Minerva Britanna, or a Garden of Heroical Devises, furnished, and adorned with Emblemes and Impresa's of sundry natures* (1612) was written and illustrated by Henry Peacham. He is thus the first English-born illustrator whose name is known. Although among his several books of popular instruction one is *The Art of Drawing with the Pen* (1606), his two hundred devices are as prosaic as his verse. Peacham illustrated an *Aesop's Fables*, but no copy is extant. His rough sketch of a scene from *Titus Andronicus* makes him in a limited sense the first illustrator of Shakespeare. The woodcut devices accompanying arms of the royal family and thirty nobles 'With Emblemes annexed, poetically unfolded' in Sir Henry Godyeare's *Mirrour of Majestie* (1618) comprise one of the few original emblem book series of the period.

18) DE PASSE, from Wither: *A Collection of Emblemes*, 198 mm.

George Wither's *A Collection of Emblemes* (1635, 1634) is the handsomest English emblem book (fig. 18). But the two hundred devices were engraved over twenty years earlier by Crispin de Passe and his family for Rollenhagen's *Nucleus Emblematum Selectissimorum* (Arnheim, 1611). In 1635 also appeared Quarles' *Emblemes* with seventy-eight devices of small children, all but two copied by William Marshall and William Simpson from Jesuit emblem books, Hugo's *Pia Desideria* (1624) and *Typus Mundi* (1627), both printed in Antwerp. The candle motif devices in Quarles' *Hieroglyphikes of the Life of Man* (1638) are also derived from abroad (fig. 19). However, the great popularity of Quarles' work through two and a half centuries did much to establish the importance of the image in conjunction with text.

Through the first part of the century travel books such as *Coryat's Crudities* (1611) by Thomas Coryat with a half-dozen engravings by William Hole, and George Sandys' *A Relation of a Journey* (1615) with engravings possibly by Francis

Tempus erit.

Will: Marshall sculpsit.

19) MARSHALL, from Quarles:
Hieroglyphikes of the Life of Man, 90 × 62 mm.

Delaram after drawings by Sandys, contain illustrations that occasionally approach being interpretive. The woodcuts in seventeenth-century broadsides do not come within our definition of book illustrations. The woodcut of the scholar Faustus calling up a hideous Mephistopheles on the title-page of Marlowe's *Doctor Faustus* (1624) is naive but genuinely illustrative.

Jan Baptist Gaspars, Abraham van Diepenbeeck, and Sir John Baptist Medina

---

The most talented book illustrator resident in England during the seventeenth century besides Cleyn, Hollar, and Barlow is Jan Baptist Gaspars (Jaspars)(1620–1691) from Antwerp. Remarkably, he also etched in the open Van Dyck style. The four plates for *Lysis, or The Extravagant Shepherd* (T. Heath, 1653), a translation of Charles Sorel's 'anti-romance' *Le Berger Extravagant* by John Davies of Kidwelly, are the frontispiece and illustrations for the first three of the fourteen chapters. The novel and the illustrations were popular, for though the British Library has copies of the 1653, 1654, and 1660 editions, the four plates occur together only as insertions in one copy (C.30.m.8) of Edward Benlowes' *Theophila* (1652).

The frontispiece (*c.* 270 × 185 mm.) for the book is a Manneristic parody, in which a pair of fashionably dressed young lovers dally before a nude female on an elevated throne, symbolizing fleshly love no doubt, while Venus and Cupid express dismay from a pedestal. The Book I pastoral scene (230 × 140 mm.) of the shepherd Lysis seated beside his sheep on the ground conversing with an elegant friend from Paris hovers wittily between realism and artificiality. The frontispiece for Book II is a portrait (235 × 166 mm.) of a lady named Charite with suns for eyes, Cupid on her brow, flowers on her cheeks, and other romantic images made literal. It represents a copperplate design that Lysis is working on. These three plates are unsigned. For Book III, 'The Banquet of the Gods', Gaspars etched, and signed in capitals 'Ianbattest Iaspers Inv: et Fec', a plate so large (260 × 332 mm.) that it has to be folded. Gods and goddesses in contemporary dress, servants with bowls of nectar, drunken Pan and satyrs, and Death are heaped together in a cross between a celebrities cocktail party and a Hollywood film orgy. During his many years in England as an assistant to Lely and Kneller, Gaspars seems never to have tried to fulfil the brilliant promise of this amusing excursion into book illustration.

One minor landmark is Elkanah Settle's *The Empress of Morocco: A Tragedy* (W. Cademan, 1673). It is not, as some have thought, the first play published in England with illustrations. A translation of Beza's *A Tragedie of Abraham's Sacrifice* (Vautrollier, 1577) with three woodcuts is a century earlier, and Elizabethan and Jacobean plays sometimes had illustrative woodcuts on their title-pages, such as the one of two men (an actor and the playwright?) explaining a morality play to a group of women in *Three Lordes and Three Ladies* (R. Jhones, 1590). In addition to a folding frontispiece of the front of The Duke's Theatre, *The Empress of Morocco* contains five engravings (112 × 96 mm.) of scenes from the play, including one of Moors dancing to African drums, a masque in Hell and a torture chamber. They are printed within repeated impressions of an engraving of the proscenium of the theatre (202 × 149 mm.) with a musicians' gallery above the stage. Though miserably engraved by W. Dolle, they were clearly based on sketches made in the theatre and give a vivid sense of what the Restoration audience looked at.

The only major English literary work with important engraved illustrations in the seventeenth century is the first illustrated edition of *Paradise Lost* (1688). The illustrator was young John Baptist Medina (*c.* 1660–1710), recently arrived from Brussels. (He went on to Edinburgh, where he became a successful portraitist and baronet.) The designs seem based on the brief prose 'Argument' or summary of the action that Milton placed at the head of each 'Book', not on a reading of the poem. The plates sometimes use the medieval continuous rep-

resentation of several incidents at different distances, as in Harington's *Orlando Furioso* and Cleyn's Ovid's *Metamorphoses*, but sometimes show only one incident (fig. 20). Medina's muscular Adam and Eve and Roman Satan reveal more regard for Rubens than for Milton. Except for the often reproduced melodramatic first illustration of Satan and the fallen angels, the designs become somewhat meagre and matter-of-fact under the burin of Michiel Burghers, an engraver from Amsterdam.

Late in the century the humble woodcuts (100 × 60 mm.) in various editions of *Pilgrim's Progress* are the first inglorious interpretations of one of the most illustrated of all English books.

William Faithorne

It is difficult to say exactly what part William Faithorne (1616?–1691) played in seventeenth-century book illustration. A student of Nanteuil and recognized as the best native-born portrait engraver of the century, he is completely inconsistent about indicating the creator of his designs. For instance, whereas on the portrait of John Milton he has written scrupulously 'Gul: Faithorne ad Vivum Delin. et Sculpsit', he is capable of omitting the name of even so prestigious a contemporary painter as Sir Peter Lely from his copy of the portrait of Abraham Cowley. Though Faithorne did a score of illustrative frontispieces, only four of the books listed in Louis Fagan's *catalogue raisonné* of Faithorne's work (1888) can be considered really illustrated. In no place does the engraver say that he invented the designs, and his name is not on many of the plates even as the engraver.

The first of the four books that Fagan lists as if illustrated by Faithorne is Jeremy Taylor's *The Great Examplar of Sanctity and Holy Life* (1653). In addition to an elaborate half-title frontispiece of Mary and the Christ Child, it contains eleven plates (*c.* 243 × 203 mm.) of the Evangelists and scenes from the life of Christ. Somewhat suspiciously, these illustrations are larger than the folio pages and have to be folded under. Faithorne signs them all as the engraver and dates some 1653, but Hollar, who was living with him in his house near Temple Bar where he also sold prints, silently etched two of them. While in exile in Paris with other Royalists, Faithorne had had the run of the immense collection of prints belonging to the Abbé Michel de Marolles. It would seem at least as likely that he should have copied these designs then as that in the midst of Puritan England he should have invented eleven traditional Catholic pictures as illustrations for Taylor's Anglican text.

For a Latin and Greek text of the poems of Moschus, Bion, and Theocritus in

20) MEDINA, from Milton: *Paradise Lost* (1688), 288 × 188 mm.

1655 Faithorne signs two plates (196 × 153 mm.) 'fecit'. He probably drew the designs himself after Continental models. In one Leander takes Hero's hand, while a suspicious duenna watches. In the other Hero is shown inelegantly diving from her tower, not into the sea but down upon the body of the drowned Leander at the water's edge.

Twenty years later for *Antiquitates Christianae: or, The History of the Life and Death of the Holy Jesus and Apostles* by Jeremy Taylor and William Cave (1675), Faithorne assembles over ninety plates – or apparently he does. He signs the frontispiece Annunciation only as the engraver. Most of the time two of the plates (104 × 70 mm.) are placed side by side at the top of the page. No less than fourteen are etchings by Hollar, though unsigned, one is signed by Robert White, and one by A.H. Once more Faithorne makes no claim that he designed any of these traditional Catholic pictures, and it is not clear how many he engraved.

Fagan includes in his catalogue the folio *Life and Death of our Blessed Lord and Saviour Jesus Christ: An Heroic Poem* (1693) by Samuel Wesley, rector of Epworth, Lincolnshire, but he offers no reason for implicitly attributing the sixty illustrations (*c.* 205 × 150 mm.) to Faithorne. Only one main plate is signed in any way, no. 41, St. Matthew, engraved by Nicholas Yeates. Some small etched martyrdoms inserted in the large engraved portraits of saints are initialled J.G. It seems apparent that several engravers were involved – Yeates and probably Faithorne for the individual figures and at least two other hands for the illustrations, one who produced superior dark almost mezzotint effects as in no. 55, 'The Descent from the Cross'. But the question of engravers is a side issue. The one Yeates signature indicates that the plates were almost certainly all engraved in England. But there is no evidence whatever as to who drew the original designs or when or where. The lack of inscription in a 5 mm. blank space at the bottom of every plate, including the one engraved by Yeates, seems suspicious. More than that, however, it is straining credulity to think that Faithorne, at the very end of his career as a reproductive portrait engraver, presumably in the year of his death at seventy-five or so and two years before the publication of the book, should make the extraordinary effort of drawing twenty figures and forty complex traditional Catholic illustrations of outmoded excellence for this poem by the father of John Wesley.

If William Faithorne did in fact invent original designs for these four books, then he must be accepted as the second native-born English book illustrator, and one of considerable technical stature. But until someone proves otherwise, we cannot give him credit for being the creative illustrator he never claimed to be.

*   *   *   *   *

Our brief review of the first two centuries of book illustration in England makes a few points clear. In spite of the absence of a single original illustrator during the first period of printing in England, under the leadership of Caxton, De Worde, and Pynson the illustrated book flourished. During the remaining three-quarters of the sixteenth century the quality of illustration sinks to a low level. Yet in addition to some isolated books of considerable interest, there are several exceptional ones, almost all from the presses of Day and Bynneman. In the seventeenth century the intaglio processes of engraving and etching displace the woodcut. Interpretive illustration declines, but a number of sumptuous illustrated folios are produced. Of the artists resident in England between the introduction of printing in 1476 and 1700 not one can be said to be a significant book illustrator except Gheeraerts, Cleyn, Hollar, and Barlow.

21) Gheeraerts, *A stag hunt*, 162 × 271 mm.

CHAPTER III

Marcus Gheeraerts the Elder and the Tradition of Aesopic Fable Illustration

I N TWO WAYS Marcus Gheeraerts the elder has a place in the history of English book illustration. First, during the years 1568 to 1577, when he worked as an artist in London, he illustrated one book and may have illustrated two others. Second, his earlier etched Aesopic illustrations directly influenced Cleyn, Hollar, and Barlow. In fact, his fable book is the main source from which traditional motifs enter England in the seventeenth century.

Marcus Gheeraerts the Elder: His Life

We have already said that the first known artist seriously to practise original book illustrating in England is Marcus Gheeraerts the elder (*c.* 1520–*c.* 1590). Son of a Bruges painter – the name is spelled Geerarts, Gerards, and other ways – he may have studied in Antwerp, possibly with Hieronymus Cock. Though he was a well respected painter, no painting wholly or unquestionably by him survives. He is one of the first artists to make etching a substantial part of his career. Though the technique was discovered early in the sixteenth century, he is one of the first artists consistently to design and etch his own plates, to use etching for extensive book illustration, and to fill his illustrations with naturalistic detail, notably of birds and animals drawn from life. He is also the first known etcher to practise in England and the first illustrator to introduce emblematic designs in a book printed in England.

Gheeraerts lives today as one of the first modern book illustrators and one of enduring appeal. His first book is the most important one. In 1567 he illustrated and had printed at his own cost in Bruges a Flemish verse version of Aesop's fables, *De warachtighe Fabulen der Dieren* (the true fables of animals). We shall consider it later. The Protestant uprising in 1566 led to brutal reprisals by the Spaniards under the Duke of Alba, and Gheeraerts, a Calvinist (though perhaps also a member of 'The Family of Love', since a number of his friends were), fled to London in March 1568 with his small son, Marcus. The son became the leading

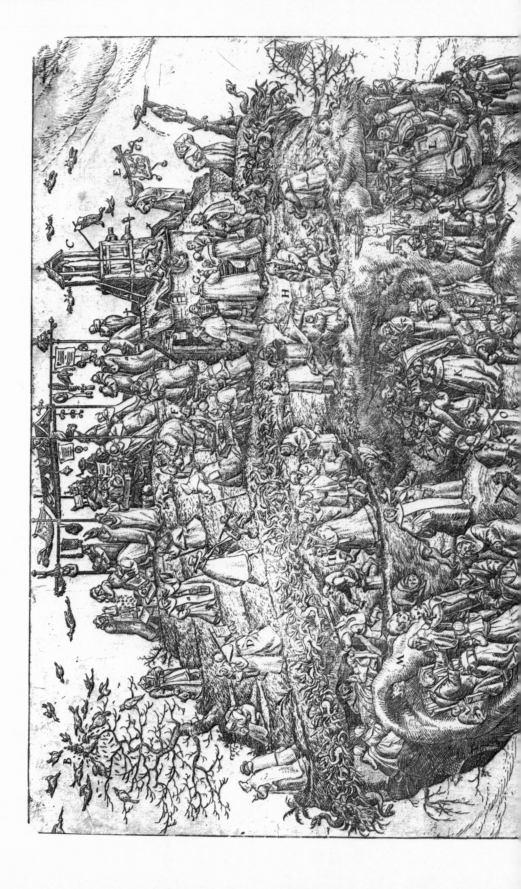

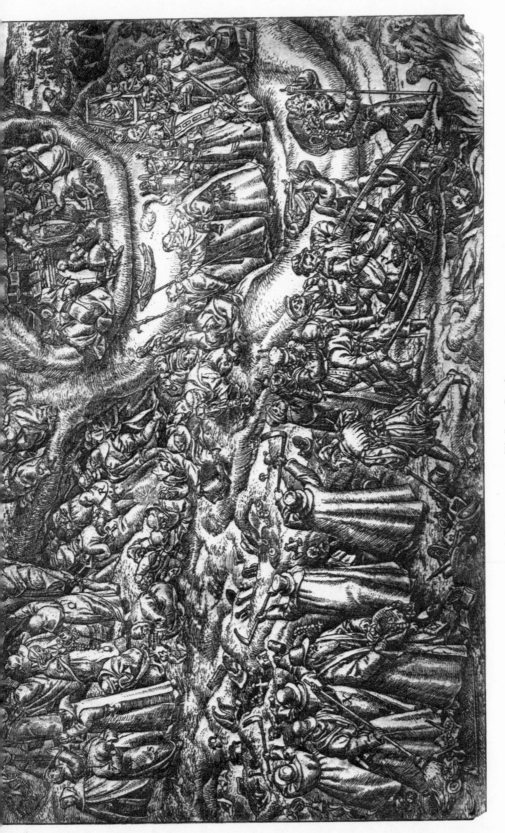

22) GHEERAERTS, *The Image Breakers*, 429 × 312 mm.

portrait painter under Elizabeth I and James I. He never etched, made prints, or illustrated books, but father and son are still being confused by critics. Later in 1568 Gheeraerts illustrated *Het Theatre* by Jan van der Noot.

Gheeraerts worked at his trade of artist in London for nine years. He married Susanna de Critz in 1571. Her father and brother were leading portrait painters, and her younger sister married Marcus the younger in 1590. Possibly the elder Gheeraerts was associated with the *atelier* of Troilus de Critz and may have painted portraits of Queen Elizabeth himself (though hardly from life), including one at Welbeck Abbey. Besides the *Theatre* etchings, only three other works by Gheeraerts can with certainty be attributed to his London years. In a letter Daniel Rogers refers to a portrait of himself, now lost. At the National Gallery of Scotland a pen and wash drawing of a stag hunt (fig. 21) is signed with Gheeraerts' monogram, B. presumably for Bruges, and F. for *fecit* and dated 1575. Then there is a long etched 'Procession of the Knights of the Garter' (1576) with Queen Elizabeth bringing up the rear and Windsor Castle in the background. Hollar adapted it in 1666, with respectful reference to Gheeraerts.

In 1577 during a lull in the persecution of heretics Gheeraerts returned to Antwerp, where Christopher Plantin and a handful of engraver entrepreneurs made the city an international centre for prints and printing in spite of the troubled times. The next year Philippe Galle published *Esbatement moral des animaux*, a French version of the 1567 *Fabulen der Dieren* with the original plates and some new ones by Gheeraerts. In 1584, still in Antwerp, Gheeraerts etched similar illustrations for Jan Moerman's Latin *Apologi creaturarum*, a fable book with emblematic elements, printed by Gerard de Jode. During his nine years in Antwerp he drew designs of varying degrees of artistic interest, which were burin engraved by others for Galle, de Jode, and other famous engraver-publishers but lost the Gheeraerts' feeling in the process. In 1586 Gheeraerts returned to London. When he died is unrecorded, but about 1590 is a plausible date.

Besides his illustrations, only four of Gheeraerts' individual etchings survive, all exceptionally large. These are a bird's-eye view of Bruges, nearly 6 feet long, in ten plates (1562), 'The Image Breakers' (1566?), 'The Procession of the Knights of the Garter' in nine plates (1576), and 'William of Orange as St. George' (1577?). The savage 'Image Breakers' is a remarkable etching (429 × 312 mm.) (fig. 22). It commemorates the vandalizing of the Catholic churches by Calvinist mobs during 1566. The Pope receives tribute on the top of a hill in the form of a dead priest's head on which at stations on the way up priests, the faithful, and apes celebrate Roman Catholic rites. At the base Calvinists destroy religious objects. The satire is ambiguous. Both as an artist whose major paintings were in Catholic churches and as a man who probably shared the enlightened views of 'The Family of Love', Gheeraerts could hardly have been enthusiastic about such violence. The etching of William the Silent as St. George slaying a dragon apparently celebrated William's stay in Antwerp (18–23 September 1577) on his way to Brussels. Later the text was altered and the print reissued when William was assassinated. The series of engravings on subjects such as animals, birds, and butterflies, the Passion, and the Labours of Hercules made by several Antwerp engravers from drawings supplied by Gheeraerts lack the appeal of his own etchings.

Book Illustration by Gheeraerts in London

We shall first look more closely at the books Gheeraerts illustrated or may have illustrated during his years in London. Then we shall return to his Bruges *Fabulen der Dieren* and the tradition of Aesopic fable illustration.

In September 1568, five months after Gheeraerts arrived in London, John Day published *Het Theatre*, a book of Dutch verse and prose by Jan van der Noot, with twenty unsigned etched illustrations (88 × 71 mm.). There can no longer be any doubt that they are by Gheeraerts. These are the first etchings known to have been made in England, and because of the nature of etchings and Gheeraerts' Flemish outlook, they are an immense advance beyond English woodcut illustrations in naturalistic detail, modelling of form, illusion of distance, and shading. This sense of reality is particularly true of the birds and animals, in which Gheeraerts excelled (fig. 23). The *Theatre* illustrations also contain emblematic elements, such as the pelican, the ship of faith, and proud monuments in ruins, long before allegorical emblem books became fashionable in England. Less tangible but not less important, Gheeraerts' illustrations convey something of the emotional content of the poems. One month later Day issued *Le Théatre*, a French edition, dedicated to Queen Elizabeth I, with the same plates. The following year Henry Bynneman brought out an English edition, usually known as *A Theatre for Voluptuous Worldlings* (1569). Edmund Spenser, then about sixteen years old, translated some of the verse and must have studied Gheeraerts' etchings as he did so. The capable facsimile woodcut copies in the 1569 edition lose the subtleties of the etchings, but the designs are by Gheeraerts.

For stylistic and circumstantial reasons it seems probable that Gheeraerts drew the designs that someone else cut for the thirty-seven woodcut illustrations in Bateman's *A Christall Glasse* (Day, 1569) and for about a hundred of those in Holinshed's *Chronicles of England, Scotlande, and Irelande* (Bynneman, 1577). *A Christall Glasse* is, like the *Theatre*, a Protestant variant of the emblem book. It

23) GHEERAERTS, from van der Noot: *Het Theatre*, 84 × 69 mm.

seems reasonable that Day would call on the same artist to illustrate it. The fresh woodcuts allegorize virtues and vices in earnest naturalistic scenes, unlike the graceful artificialities of the standard emblem book but like the fusion of fable and emblem matter in some of the designs for *Fabulen der Dieren* and the later *Apologi creaturarum*. Above each cut are two or four lines of doggerel verse about the characteristic discussed, and below the cut is a prose 'Signification' explaining the illustration in emblem-book style and therefore written after the drawing was made. Beneath the cut for Gluttony (fig. 24) the 'Signification' reads: 'These which are fightyng, signifieth incontinence: he which is slaine hazarde: and death: and the one which goeth out with his sword in hys hand *audax*, one past grace, or a murtherer.'

Similarly, Gheeraerts is the most logical artist for the daunting job of drawing the designs for about a hundred of the hundred and thirty-eight several-sized woodcuts in the first edition of Raphaell Holinshed's *Chronicles of England, Scotlande, and Irelande* (1577), which Bynneman printed for John Harrison. The rest of the woodcuts, battle scenes and similar generally applicable designs, do

24) GHEERAERTS, from Bateman: *A Christall Glasse*, 95 × 112 mm.

not seem cut especially for this book. The woodcuts precisely designed to illustrate Holinshed's text are remarkable interpretations of complex historical scenes. (Their effectiveness is diminished by the presence of the miscellaneous blocks, variations in sizes, and unfortunate repetition to give over a thousand impressions.) They cover a fascinating range of subjects – hunts, executions, councils, feasts, musicians, building construction, cities and ships burning, naval and land battles, and Macbeth and Banquo encountering the weird sisters – before Shakespeare encountered Holinshed. A comparison of the woodcut of a stag hunt (fig. 25) with the hunt drawing at the National Gallery of Scotland (fig. 21) which was brought to my attention in 1972 by Mr. Keith K. Andrews, Keeper of the Department of Prints and Drawings, provides strong support for my hypothesis, first offered in 1971, that Gheeraerts made the drawings for the original Holinshed woodcuts.

In their immense variety of subject and treatment, often revealing close reading of the text, selection of non-obvious moments, inclusion of authentic accessory detail not provided by Holinshed, vigorous handling of individual figures and

25) GHEERAERTS (attrib.), from Holinshed:
Chronicles of England, Scotlande, and Irelande, 78 × 132 mm.

groups, and realization of dramatic effects, the original Holinshed woodcuts surpass any made in England before 1700 except Foxe's *Actes and Monuments* series and six of the twelve in Derricke's *Image of Irelande*. If my attribution of the Holinshed designs to Gheeraerts is correct, they add immensely to his record as the first known interpretive illustrator of books printed in England. If I am wrong, Holinshed's *Chronicles of England, Scotlande, and Irelande* is still one of the monumental achievements of English book illustration.

Aesopic Fables

Aesop's Fables has always been a fictive title. Aesop never wrote any fables; there has never been one definitive collection of Aesopic fables, and there is none now. Bestiaries, brief didactic narratives with animal characters metaphorically acting out human dilemmas, have existed in all societies from immemorial times. Apparently in the sixth century B.C. an actual Aesop, a slave from Thrace, achieved local fame as a teller of animal fables in the service of a man named Iadmon on the island of Samos and so secured his freedom. Thereafter in succeeding centuries legend added details. He was dumb, ugly, and humpbacked, but a goddess gave him speech. He was a native of Phrygia, Asia Minor, a few miles from Samos. He won his freedom and travelled widely, telling fables and solving problems, until the inhabitants of Delphi falsely accused him of stealing a cup from the temple of Apollo and pushed him off a cliff to his death. The traditional Life of Aesop is fiction, but it serves as a convenient device to strengthen the pretence that Aesop was the author of all the fables that were popular in classical times, as we know best because Socrates whiled away the time before his execution turning some of the fables into verse.

Based on a lost manuscript by Demetrius of Phalerum (*c.* 300 B.C.), in the Christian era Aesopic fables were collected, put into writing, and circulated. The chief collections, in verse, are those by Phaedrus written in Latin (*c.* 40) and those in Greek by Babrius shortly after that date. A Latin prose version of the Phaedrus collection was passed on by Romulus between the years 350 and 600, and a Latin verse version of a number from the Babrius collection by Avianus (*c.* 400). Also derived from Demetrius of Phalerum, the Life of Aesop has come down mainly from manuscripts by Maximus Planudes (*c.* 1300) and Rinuccio da Castiglione of Arezzo (1448). Thereafter these manuscript collections were copied, turned into prose, translated, revised, paraphrased, and augmented by fables from the Orient. Furthermore, from the Renaissance on there were fresh inventions by gentlemen whose education might have included exercises in writing fables. (*Fabule Esopi cum commento* was a standard Renaissance schoolbook.) Among the innovators who have written their own fables in modern dress, however, only Jean de la Fontaine has achieved universal acceptance.

The fables of Aesop are as English as most of the tales of Chaucer or the plays of Shakespeare. In paraphrase, imitation, and allusion they permeate English literature. More surely than Odysseus or Don Quixote the wise ex-slave has become naturalized, and the fables written in Aesop's name have pleased many generations of adults and children. From the beginning of printing to the present, editions meant for general reading have commonly been illustrated.

John J. McKendry of the Metropolitan Museum of Art in *Aesop: Five Centuries of Illustrated Fables* explains the popularity of the fables with illustrators: 'The simplicity of the stories specifies no circumstantial detail . . . and, very important, there is no definitive text'. These two conditions, taken together with the universal familiarity with the fables individually and as a form, have given illustrators a unique freedom. The elemental incidents led to inevitable basic motifs in the first incunabula woodcuts. Then all over Europe a body of similar illustrations evolved as artists copied, rearranged, and recreated these prototypes to fit the fables chosen by their editors. A dozen or so English *Aesops* rank as notable illustrated books, and among these the fable books illustrated by Wenceslaus Hollar and Francis Barlow are the most distinguished.

The Transmission of Motifs

Before we look at Gheeraerts' fable illustrations, a brief account of the tradition of Aesopic fable illustration as it reaches seventeenth-century England through Gheeraerts is desirable.

First, however, it is necessary to say something about the ideas of motifs, transmission, and degrees of indebtedness underlying our discussion. The motif, as the term is used here, is the essential action or arrangement of the chief figures or other elements in an illustration. If in the fable of the fox and the crow the fox sits on the ground looking up at the crow in a tree with a morsel of food in its mouth, that is the motif. If the fox is shown walking off with the morsel or some other significant change occurs, that is a different motif. If less significant change occurs – the fox stands instead of sits, for example – the motif is only modified. The manner of treatment, as the life-likeness of the fox and the crow or the choice of background detail, does not affect the designation of the motif. It may, however, significantly affect the expressiveness of the interpretation.

Because the fable is usually concentrated into a single situation with one obvious means of representation – the fox sitting on the ground looking up at the crow with the morsel in its mouth in the instance just used – illustrators, as can be seen in very early manuscripts, tend to conceive similar motifs. Then, too, before 1700 the idea of plagiarism, that borrowing the motif of a painting or an illustration is unimaginative, unethical, or even illegal, was not generally accepted. Borrowing fable-illustration motifs was an open transaction. Whether it was an act of admiration, expedience, larceny, or something of all three can rarely be known now. A great deal of borrowing is mechanical tracing. To the cutter of a wood-block, it is all the same whether he cuts a fresh original design or a copy of an old one. The drawing has to be made on the block, whether the artist, the woodcutter, or a third hand puts it there.

Only fitfully does the fable illustrator respond to a particular text. (He has to if the fable is a new invention or is significantly altered.) Only rarely, as editions of Aesopic fables proliferate throughout Europe, does an artist impose a new face on traditional motifs or change them in meaningful ways. The editions illustrated by these few innovators are the key sources in tracing the transmission of motifs. Thus in a separate study I have been able to record the descent of each of the motifs in the illustrations of Gheeraerts, Cleyn, Hollar, and Barlow from its first occurrence in a printed book (as far as I have been able to discover) and indicate the source and degree of indebtedness of each occurrence. In the course of this analysis it has been possible to observe how imaginative a few illustrators have been not only in creating new motifs and restructuring old ones but also in revitalizing old ones borrowed without significant change.

The Tradition of Aesopic Fable Illustration before Gheeraerts

---

The origins of Aesopic illustration go back to the drawings in manuscripts of the several collections of fables from which the principal printed editions were drawn. Our account begins with the first dated illustrated printed book, Ulrich Boner's *Der Edelstein* (Albrecht Pfister, Bamberg, 1461). At first anonymous hands copy and modify traditional motifs taken from manuscripts and *Edelstein* and invent new ones. Then known artists, beginning with Bernard Salomon in our sequence, follow the same procedure. After Pfister's the following are the key editions before Gheeraerts': Johann Zainer (Ulm, *c.* 1476), Denys Janot (Paris, 1542), Bernard Salomon for Jean de Tournes (Lyon, 1547, etc.), Christopher Plantin (Antwerp, 1565), and Virgil Solis for Sigmund Feyerabend (Frankfurt, 1566).

Fourteen motifs from emblem books are absorbed in that part of the Aesopic tradition that we are tracing. The sequence is from the first illustrated edition of Alciati's *Emblematum liber* printed by Heinrich Steyner (Augsburg, 1531) through Chrestien Wechel (Paris, 1534), Bernard Salomon for Jean de Tournes (Lyon, 1547), and Geoffroy Ballain for Christopher Plantin (Antwerp, 1565). Marcus Gheeraerts then draws motifs from both fable and emblem streams for his *De warachtighe Fabulen der Dieren* (Bruges, 1567).

Ulrich Boner was a Dominican monk of Berne, Switzerland, who in the four-teenth century translated into German verse a hundred Aesopic fables from Avianus and other collections. Pfister's 1461 edition of Boner's *Der Edelstein* con-tains a hundred and one woodcuts (his undated edition has two more) without doubt based on non-extant manuscript drawings. They have a great deal of primitive charm, but beyond that most of them present the essential point of the fables with marvellous boldness and economy. They fulfil superbly the function of illustration, as in the woodcut for the fable of 'The Lion & the Mouse' (fig. 26). Yet the *Edelstein* illustrations have been neglected, even disparaged by eminent authorities.

The two hundred or so woodcuts in the *Vita Esopi et fabulae,* collected and edited by Dr. Heinrich Steinhöwel (Johann Zainer, Ulm, *c.* 1476), have been un-reservedly praised by the same authorities. They present the essential characters of the fables with admirable directness, but, impertinent as it may be to say so, they seem more literal, more laboured, less imaginative than the *Edelstein* series (fig. 27). Of the Zainer motifs fifty-one seem based on *Edelstein*. (In one design Zainer's man follows Pfister's in the error of drawing a lion where there should be a boar.) The rest of the Zainer designs undoubtedly come from manuscript drawings. The edition was tremendously popular. The woodcuts reappear in a

26) Anon, from Boner: *Der Edelstein* (Albrecht Pfister 1461), 81 × 111 mm.

27) Anon, from Steinhowel: *Vita Esopi et Fabulae* (Johann Zainer c. 1476), 76 × 102 mm.

score of later editions, and they were widely copied in facsimile. Caxton's series is taken from a Lyon set of copies of the cuts in Sorg's Augsburg edition.

The anonymous artist who designed a hundred small woodcuts for Giles Corrozet's French collection, *Les fables du tresancien Esope, Phrygien,* printed by Denys Janot (Paris, 1542), seems to be the key person in diverting the stream of Aesopic illustration that we are following from Gothic realism to Italianate elegance. His immediate sources were diverse, but of the eighty-nine Janot motifs that are in the Gheeraerts-to-Barlow corpus, forty-six seem derived from Zainer. The large simple figures that fill the foreground of the German blocks with only the roughest indications of trees, rocks, and houses to give them a sense of place are supplanted by scenes, usually landscapes, in which the actors are shown in midground. Decorative composition, with rhythmic lines and effective management of white space, comes before narration or expressiveness (fig. 28). The four

28) ANON, from Corrozet: *Les fables du Tresancien Esope, Phrygien,* 30 × 49 mm.

artists that we are dealing with seem not to have been acquainted with Janot's series, except through the derivative work of Bernard Salomon, who designed for the Lyon printer Jean de Tournes and his associates, beginning with Corrozet's *Les fables d'Esope Phrygien* (1547). Salomon used Janot's motifs but re-drew the designs freely to achieve greater elegance and Mannerist effects (fig. 29). In later editions he added motifs not borrowed from Janot.

29) SALOMON, from Corrozet: *Les fables d'Esope Phrygien,* 36 × 47 mm.

Christopher Plantin issued a Latin *Aesopi Phrygis, et aliorum fabulae* (Antwerp, 1565) with seventy woodcut facsimiles of Salomon's designs and six blocks from Plantin's emblem books. The cutting of the Aesop blocks is poor (he bought the series from another Antwerp printer), but the designs are identical with Salomon's. Later copyists may have been looking at Plantin's edition, but they were really using Salomon's adaptations of Janot's motifs.

Virgil Solis brings back to Germany the Zainer motifs in their Italianate transformations. Solis, a master draughtsman, prepared a hundred and sixty-seven beautiful woodcuts for *Aesopi Phrygis fabule*, printed by Feyerabend, Rab, and Han (Frankfurt, 1566). Of these, a hundred and six motifs belong in the list of those found in Gheeraerts' or our English Aesops. Solis borrowed about three-quarters of these designs from Salomon and one-quarter from Zainer. It is certain that he used Salomon's designs, not Plantin's, because he died before Plantin's edition appeared. It is not certain what version of Zainer's series he used because he completely Italianized the angular German designs. Handsome as the Solis series is, conceptually it is utterly unoriginal.

The *Aesopic Fable Illustrations of Marcus Gheeraerts – Bruges* (*1567*), *Antwerp* (*1578*)

In publishing *De warachtighe Fabulen der Dieren* (Pieter de Clerck, 1567) in his native Bruges with a title-page design and a hundred and seven etched illustrations (*c.* 94 × 112 mm.), Gheeraerts was fully conscious that he was giving traditional Aesopic fable illustration a new image. He also bragged modestly that the text by his friend Edewaerd de Dene, a Bruges lawyer, was written for the first time in 'Flemish or Dutch verse . . . adorned with biblical phrases and instructive examples'. Yet perhaps because he was working on the plates while de Dene was rewriting the fables, Gheeraerts makes no effort to give his illustrations a religious tone. He has no change of attitude when eleven years later in Antwerp he adds eighteen new plates to the hundred and seven for *Esbatement moral des animaux* (Gerard Smits for Philippe Galle, 1578) with the French text apparently by Pieter Heyns. In 1579 Galle published *Mythologia ethica*, a Latin version by Arnold Freitag with the same plates. The plates are also found in a number of later editions, worn and retouched by gravers, as late as the eighteenth century. They are the sources of other series in Holland, Czechoslovakia, France, and Germany, as well as in England.

Gheeraerts drew widely on his predecessors but mainly on Solis for sixty-one motifs and Salomon for twenty-one. Up to thirty of his motifs seem original. He accepted the traditional motifs but introduced complexities of concept related to his Flemish outlook and refinements of execution natural to his etching needle.

In the plates of the *Fabulen der Dieren* and *Esbatement moral des animaux* series he elaborated with fresh inventiveness the standard elements of the simple fable incidents. A first-rate draughtsman, he used the freedom that etching allows to treat his chief figures in realistic detail and to establish them as credible inhabitants of their naturalistic environment. He neither idealizes nor degrades his characters, human or otherwise, and never inflicts on his non-human creatures the indignities of later anthropomorphism. He delights in filling the middle ground with rural and town scenes of independent charm: thatched cottages, peasants walking along lonely roads, walled towns like Bruges surrounded by water on which boats float placidly, and occasionally for bravura a great round Roman ruin in the fashionable Italianate manner of Antwerp artists like Cock and Frans Floris. His superiority as a book illustrator over more talented artists arises from the easy way that he reveals his characters as intensely involved in the action within scenes of lively but subordinate interest.

30) GHEERAERTS, from de Dene, *De warachtighe Fabulen der Dieren*, 94 × 112 mm.

Gheeraerts' representation of the fox and the goat in a well exemplifies how he contributed to the development of fable illustrations (fig. 30). In his small block (34 × 42 mm.) Salomon shows the goat in a circular well with a rope and pulley attached to a right-angle support (fig. 31). The fox stands on a square stone with his fore-feet on the rim of the well and peers over at the goat. Nearby is the corner of a thatched barn and a bit of ruined wall over a low arch. In his larger woodcut (48 × 69 mm.) Solis copies exactly Salomon's central action (and it prints in reverse). In the background he adds a vague building and a meaningless ruin. Gheeraerts revisualizes – and revitalizes – the entire scene. He apparently took his cue from Salomon and put the fox on the top of a stone arch (Solis' arch is earthen). The fox peers down three steps at the handsome buck in a well with low sides. Just beyond the well a man serenely poles a boat in the water beneath the high walls of a town like Bruges. Old piles stick out of the water, a characteristic touch of Flemish realism. The tiny figures of two idlers look down from the wall, and through an arch distant buildings catch the light. The improbability of the circumstances of the fable and the position of the well is dissipated by the utter believability of the animals and the scene that enfolds them.

De warachtighe Fabulen der Dieren is a landmark in popular illustration. Gheeraerts deserves a place in the history of book illustration for his early use of etching instead of engraving as a sophisticated substitute for woodcuts and for his initiative in widening the scope of book illustration. He was instrumental in establishing plastic etching instead of rigid engraving as the medium of the best English illustration of the seventeenth century, in spite of the fashion for engraved portraits and strapwork title-pages. Most of all, he set a high standard for illustration as a story-telling vehicle and as a work of art. Gheeraerts moves the Aesopic illustrations into the full naturalistic tide of modern book illustration. Indeed, his Aesop plates make him one of the shapers of the modern European style that endures to this day.

31) SALOMON, from Corrozet, *Les fables d'Esope Phrygien*, 35 × 46 mm.

CHAPTER IV

Francis Cleyn and John Ogilby

THE SECOND of Barlow's known predecessors also has a place in this account. He is Francis Cleyn (Clein) (1582–1657/58). Though born in Rostock, Mecklenburg-Schwerin, Cleyn spent the greater part of his professional career in England, and his hundred and seventy-five or so illustrations appear in English books spanning nearly thirty years. Cleyn, who had studied for four years in Rome and Venice, spent about eight years in the employ of King Christian IV of Denmark. The Italianate narrative paintings he did for 'Rosenborg', the King's country-seat on the outskirts of Copenhagen, and other royal palaces are figure-filled and several-planed. Before James I died in 1625, he brought Cleyn to England. Charles I made him chief designer of the royal tapestry factory at Mortlake near Richmond. Much of the credit for the high reputation of Mortlake tapestries throughout Europe must be Cleyn's. Three of his children, Francis, John, and Penelope, were also artists. His other pupils include Josiah English and William Dobson. At Mortlake under Cleyn's direction the sons copied the five Raphael cartoons for the great 'Miraculous Draught of the Fishes' tapestries now on loan at the Victoria and Albert Museum. In later years Cleyn seems to have lived in Covent Garden, where he is buried at St. Paul's.

Though much esteemed by Charles I, Cleyn suffered from the money problems that plagued Mortlake. He continued his association with the factory until his death but supplemented his income in other ways. He did decorative paintings for rooms, the grotesque panels at Ham House being still preserved. He also turned to illustration and designed frontispieces, title-pages, ornaments, and prints, such as the three series, 'Septem liberales artes' (1645) (123 × 101 mm.), 'Quinque sensuum descriptio' (1646) (86 × 169 mm.), and 'Paedopaegnion . . . Designes of Frizes, with Boyes, Beasts and Fruits Usefull for Painters Goldsmiths Carvers &c' (1650) (c. 50 × 150 mm.).

Among Cleyn's independent prints one etching, Dido and Aeneas in modern dress, probably made in Copenhagen, is a graphic joke. (At 'Rosenborg' he painted a surrealist head made up of kitchen utensils.) A fashionable couple from a dispersed hunt struggle on foot toward a cave in a heavy rain, which is controlled and amplified by seven cloud-borne putti. In the mouth of the cave are Juno and her peacock. Above is the caption, straight from *Punch*, 'Guare l'Eau la bas'. It is a lively design (194 × 158 mm.), but the execution is uncertain. The signature 'F.C. in. et fe.', as well as the etching, makes this plate the key in identifying work that Cleyn may have etched himself.

Ovid's Metamorphoses (*1632*)

Cleyn's first substantial book illustrations are those for George Sandys' translation of Ovid's *Metamorphoses*, a folio printed by John Lichfield of Oxford (1632). The full title gives prominence to the illustrations: *Ovid's Metamorphosis* [sic] *Englished, Mythologiz'd, and Represented in Figures*. In addition to an engraved title-page frontispiece (based on but not copied from the one by Thomas Cecill in the 1626 edition) and a portrait frontispiece, there are fifteen engraved illustrations (*c.* 235 × 172 mm.), one for each book. Only no. 3 (fig. 32) is signed – 'Sa. Saueri scul', 'F. Clein fe.' The use of *fecit* in the sense of *inuenit* with *sculpsit* is unusual. Since these two names are also on the title-page frontispiece, and the style is constant throughout, there can be no doubt that Cleyn drew all of the illustrations and Savery engraved them. Salomon Savery of Amsterdam seems to have worked on these plates during a visit to England.

Cleyn seems familiar with the traditional illustrations for this popular classic, but I have not discovered a source for his designs. They are based on the text, not just on the argument at the beginning of each book. He follows the archaic formula of crowding into each design as many as possible of the incidents mentioned in each book, with the figures diminishing in size in receding planes. Yet, in spite of the stiffness of Savery's engraving, Cleyn's literal visualizations of the strange doings in the *Metamorphoses* must have been thoroughly welcome to English readers. They are not unwelcome today. Such transformations as Daphne in the act of turning into a laurel, Cycnus to a swan, and Acteon to a stag are the sort of events that are susceptible to illustration. The 1632 series, though lacking in inspiration, is a landmark in English book illustration, the earliest major seventeenth-century series, engraved on metal, and possibly original. The portrait and illustrations were borrowed for a Paris Latin edition (1637) prepared by the schoolmaster-scholar Thomas Farnaby for Aegidius Morel, but they returned to London for Hebb's edition (1640).

Cleyn next contributed etched frontispieces to Richard Brome's *Lachrymae Musarum* (1649) and Thomas Fuller's *A Pisgah-sight of Palestine* (1650). The 'F Clein Fe:' on the first is identical in lettering with the 'F Clein inu.' of the second, and both are similar to the 'F.C. in. et fe.' on the 'Guare l'Eau la bas' plate. The style of the two frontispieces also shows them to be by the same hand. It becomes apparent that it was Cleyn's custom up to 1654 to etch his plates but to turn them over to others to be engraved.

Cleyn's etched plate (157 × 85 mm.) for Brome's *Lachrymae Musarum,* a collection of elegies upon the death of young Henry Lord Hastings, is as lugubrious as the title. Above six lines of engraved Latin verse a shrouded soul rises from a burial urn surrounded by the nine grieving muses. The etched frontispiece (293 × 178 mm.) for Fuller's folio work on the Holy Land, *A Pisgah-sight of Palestine,* is made up of several panels of pleasantly naturalistic rural activities, such as wine-pressing and churning, surrounding a larger paradisial scene of animals with a round tower in the background. Cleyn's etching (as is customary, lightly bitten and partly burin engraved) has an attractive sketchiness about it, but his technique lacks finish. The folio also contains a number of maps and diagrams engraved by Marshall, Cross, Vaughan, and Goddard. In Book 4 an etched double spread displays nineteen figures representing 'Jewish habits' [costumes] – infant, 'soldgier', Pharisee, maidens dancing, harlot, etc. – signed 'J. Fuller fecit'.

John Ogilby (1600–1676)

We now come to a remarkable figure, John Ogilby. Because books written and published by him involve illustrations by Cleyn, Hollar, and Barlow, we shall first look at his entire career and then discuss his books as we come to them, beginning with those illustrated by Cleyn.

Ogilby, born in Scotland at Kirriemuir near Dundee, came to London between 1603 and 1606 when his father followed James I south. He missed a formal education, perhaps because his father gambled away his estate. His friend John Aubrey says that in 1612 at the age of twelve or thirteen the boy 'by his own Industry (Spangles, needles)' earned money that gained his parents' release from debtors' prison in Southwark through his father's lucky draw in a Virginia Plantation lottery. He began an apprenticeship to a Mr. Draper, a dancing-master in Gray's Inn Lane (now Road), but his public dancing career ended in 1621 when he became lame 'high-dancing' in a Jonson masque organized by the Duke of Buckingham. Yet at twenty-nine he was admitted to the Merchant-Taylors' Company, evidence of unusual personal qualities, and later he set up his own dancing school in Gray's Inn Lane.

In 1633 he went to Dublin as a gentleman of the household of the Lord-Deputy of Ireland, Viscount Thomas Wentworth, later the Earl of Strafford. He seems to

Sa Sauerÿ sculp.   Lib: 3.   F. Clein fec.

have been part of Wentworth's plan to make Dublin a fashionable capital. In addition to whatever attention he may have given dancing and other activities, he was soon engaged in building and managing the first professional theatre in Ireland in (St.) Werbergh Street, close to the Castle and a few yards from where Jonathan Swift was born in 1667. When plague closed the London theatres between May 1636 and October 1637, Ogilby was able to attract to Dublin some of the best actors and musicians of the English stage. They included James Shirley, who between 1636 and 1640, besides putting on his own plays and writing prologues, must have influenced Ogilby in a number of ways – at this time Ogilby began to paraphrase Aesop's fables in verse and to study Latin. The Lord-Deputy was so pleased with the success of Ogilby's theatre that on his own authority he gave him the title of Master of the Revels for Ireland. But the beheading of Strafford in 1641 and the Irish Rebellion left both the theatre and Ogilby's second career in ruins.

After being shipwrecked on his way back to England, he turned up penniless in Cambridge in 1647 and there in his late forties mastered Latin. He then began a literary career with his translation of Virgil's works (1649). This was followed by his verse *Aesop Paraphras'd* (1651), his first illustrated book and the link between Gheeraerts, Hollar, and Barlow. By 1654 he was able to buy a house at the end of King's Head Court off the west side of Shoe Lane, turn publisher, and issue a revised edition of the Virgil, his first illustrated folio and the first English book to finance expensive illustrations by subscription. In 1658 he edited and published a Latin Virgil, and in 1660 after some years of studying Greek, said to have been under David Whitfield, an usher in the school Shirley had set up in Whitefriars, he brought out an illustrated folio translation of Homer's *Iliad*. In the same year he first revealed an interest in geographical matters in the illustrations for a sumptuous edition of the Bible.

With the Restoration Ogilby's fortunes picked up. He was put in charge of planning the procession of Charles II to his coronation and wrote a verse account of it – *The Relation of His Majestie's Entertainment Passing through the City of London to His Coronation* (T. Roycroft for R. Marriott, 1661), reissued later with splendid engravings of arches along the route, and etchings by Hollar for an added account of the coronation. He was appointed again, this time by the King himself, Master of the Revels for Ireland. He built another Dublin theatre in Smock Alley, which opened in October 1662, and somehow managed to oversee its affairs and his London publishing with the help of William Morgan, his wife's grandson. The King also gave him the empty French title of 'Master of the Royal Imprimerie'. In 1665 Ogilby published his folio translation of the *Odyssey* and a folio edition of his *Aesop Paraphras'd*, both with commentary and impressive illus-

32) CLEYN, from *Ovid's Metamorphosis Englished*, trans. Sandys, 243 × 178 mm.

trations. But the Plague of 1665 caused difficulties, and then the Great Fire brought disaster again. Ogilby lost his house and with it his main stock of books and what was to be his master work, *Carolies*, an epic on Charles I that he had been writing for years. Schuchard says it is not clear whether he was still in King's Head Court or had moved across Fleet Street to Whitefriars Lane, now Lombard Street. Her evidence about rebuilding suggests the latter site, which she says was actually what is now 8–10 Bouverie Street with access then from Lombard Street.

Penniless again at sixty-six but supported by his courage and the faith in his undertakings that he inspired in others, Ogilby rebuilt his business. In 1668 he reissued the folio *Aesop Paraphras'd* together with *Aesopics*, a new collection of fables, and two other works, *Androcleus* and *The Ephesian Matron*, all in one volume. He had such success that he 'seemed to tread air', but he was soon out-moded by cleverer, wittier, more cynical poets and playwrights. His appoint-ment, with William Morgan, to survey the boundary lines of property in the burned area of the city and his face-saving belief that 'Rhime doggerel was ousting grave Poesie' led him to end his career as translator, poet, and publisher of poetry and in his seventies to enter an entirely new one as editor and publisher of geographic works. He was able to establish a press of his own in his house in Whitefriars Lane and to begin issuing a series of ambitious volumes. In 1671 the King bestowed on him the rodomontade title 'His Majesty's Cosmographer and Geographick Printer', without pay but with the privilege of printing maps and charts with accompanying texts, and he is today chiefly recalled by the tag 'the Royal Cosmographer'. The chief of these geographic folios contain maps and descriptive accounts of China (1669), Africa (1670), Japan (1670), America (1671), and Asia (1673) supplied by a Dutch associate, Jacob van Meurs. *Britannia* (1675) and a project for a five-volume atlas were not completed by Ogilby or Morgan, his successor as Royal Cosmographer.

In 1676 Ogilby died and was buried in the printers' church of St. Bride's, where that other great publisher of illustrated books, Wynkyn de Worde lies. An extraordinary man, John Ogilby. One can only quote Aubrey: 'He had such an excellent and prudentiall Witt, and master of so good addresse, that when he was undon he could not only shift handsomely (which is a great mastery) but he would make such rationall proposalls that would be embraced by rich and great men, that in a short time he could gaine a good Estate again, and never failed in any thing he ever undertooke but allwayes went through with profits and glorie.' Because of the typographical integrity of his folios and the importance he at-tached to their illustration, together with his close association with Cleyn, Hollar, and Barlow, Ogilby has for us a special claim to be celebrated as one of the prime forces in English book illustration.

Ogilby's Fables of Aesop Paraphras'd in Verse *(1651)*

Ogilby's first venture in illustrated books is his quarto *The Fables of Aesop Paraphras'd in Verse, and adorn'd with Sculpture*, printed by Thomas Warren for Andrew Crook (1651). It came out at the end of the year because Sir William Davenant (later to be Ogilby's unsuccessful rival for the patent of Master of the Revels for Ireland and manager of the second Dublin theatre) dates his complimentary verse 'From the Tower/Sep. 30, 1651'. (The licence reads: 'Imprimatur: Na: Brent July 1, 1651'.) To call these versions paraphrases is misleading. Like *The Canterbury Tales* they are original treatments of familiar themes. Ogilby gives free play to his imagination as he retells the fables with so many amplifications of homely detail and classical allusions that what would ordinarily have been eighty-one pages or a little more becomes two hundred and thirty-six. Uninhibited, his verse varies from fable to fable in line length, rhyme scheme, stanza form, and number of stanzas.

Dryden and Pope ridiculed Ogilby's poetry. Occasionally he descends to doggerel, but in the main he is fluent enough, unassumingly amusing rather than laboriously witty, sometimes mock-heroic, and always surprisingly colloquial. Not only does he send the fable off on new vectors, as into scholarship in the first fable of the cock that found a precious stone on a dunghill; in writing the moral, he often makes some unexpected applications. In the first fable, for instance, his moral is not unusual, but it is fresh. In place of the traditional moral – to one who is hungry, an inedible gem is worthless – he writes:

Voluptuous men Philosophie despise;
Down with all learning the arm'd Soldier cries:
On glebe and Cattell, greedy Farmers look;
And Merchants only prize their counting book.

Although Ogilby had strong Royalist connections, his few apparent references to the Civil War, in 'The Parliament of Birds' and 'The Rebellion of the Hands and Feet' for instance, are discreet and conclude with generalized morals. Ogilby was at heart a humanist, a modest follower of Erasmus and predecessor of H. G. Wells. He really wanted to instruct, to uplift. The quatrain he had engraved in the cartouche below Cleyn's frontispiece of Aesop not merely surrounded by birds and animals but talking to human beings puts his aim clearly and pays generous tribute to the power of illustrations:

Examples are best Precepts; And a Tale
Adorn'd with Sculpture better may prevaile
To make Men lesser Beasts, than all the store
Of tedious Volumes, vext the World before.

And Ogilby refers to 'these Apologues of Aesop' (using the term for fable derived from the Latin, as in the title *Apologi creaturarum*) as containing 'exemplary precepts of vertue and morality, equally accommodated to the generous and heroick spirits of noble youth, as well as the more serious studies of the grave and judicious'. Ogilby lagged behind the great Jean de la Fontaine in wit, but he preceded him by seventeen years in time.

Although Cleyn signed only the frontispiece of Aesop telling his fables, there can be no doubt that he is both designer and etcher (with considerable use of a graver) of the frontispiece portrait of Ogilby and all of the illustrations in the 1651 *Aesop Paraphras'd*. The style is similar to that of the *Lachrymae Musarum* and other signed plates. In addition to the same graceless line work, characterless faces, and fine-line engraved cross-hatching on walls and similar spaces, Cleyn's etchings are marked by stippling to supplement lined shading. His backgrounds are sometimes under-bitten.

This first Ogilby quarto edition of the 'old Philosopher in modern and Poeticall dress' has eighty illustrations (*c.* 145 × 90 mm.) printed on sheets separate from the text, one for each fable except that the related illustrations for nos. 14 and 15 are on one plate. Over half (forty-six) of Cleyn's designs are clearly borrowed from the motifs in a complete collection of Gheeraerts' illustrations. Cleyn borrowed eight from other sources, and the rest he adjusted or invented to meet new situations created by Ogilby. Cleyn is an early instance of an illustrator whose conscience was troubled by plagiarism. He rarely reproduces a source exactly, although the hart admiring his reflection in a fountain is close to Gheeraerts' version.

Apart from concealing his borrowing, Cleyn often has to incorporate a few extra details added by Ogilby, such as the scholars at work in the illustration for 'The Cock and the Precious Stone' and French and Spanish costumes on the two animals in 'The Fox and the Ape' (fig. 59). Either he read the text carefully, or Ogilby coached him. For instance in his design for the fox and goat (fig. 33) in a well the fox leaps off the goat's horns, a motif used by Zainer but changed by Salomon, Solis, and Gheeraerts to one in which the fox peers back down at the goat after getting out. But the unusual posture of the goat is the clue that Cleyn follows Ogilby's text and reinvents Zainer's motif:

Let your chin meet Your hairy Bosome [says the Fox]
that your horns may rise Upright, as if prepar'd to
But[t] the Skies: Then from your back to those
Spires Ile leap, Whence out is but a step.

Another example is 'The Battaile of the Frog and Mouse', in which Ogilby improvises on the theme for several pages. In high good spirits he puns about the

33) CLEYN, from Ogilby: *The Fables of Aesop Paraphras'd* (1651), 136 × 90 mm.

mock-heroic encounter between Frogpadock, King of the Phrogians, and Moustapha, King of the Miceans. Moustapha arrives for the joust borne in a mousetrap as in a sedan chair, a bit of fun that Cleyn dutifully takes note of (fig. 34). After the kite swoops and carries off both the champions, Ogilby draws the moral without pointed local reference:

> *Thus Pettie Princes strive with mortall hate,*
> *Till both are swallow'd by a neighbouring state.*
> *Thus factions with a civill War imbru'd*
> *By some unseen Aspirer are subdu'd.*

34) CLEYN, from *The Fables of Aesop Paraphras'd*, 148 × 92 mm.

There is ample evidence that Cleyn was a good draughtsman, even, on occasion of birds and animals. But whatever excellence his Aesop drawings may have had, it did not extend to his compositions or to the addition of imaginative realizing detail, particularly of the sort that would reinforce Ogilby's modernization of the fables. Probably the drawings were better than they seem, and most of the loss is due to Cleyn's own etching. Still, this is the first illustrated edition of Aesop of any consequence published in England since Caxton's and Pynson's. And, as we have already said, it is the bridge between Gheeraerts' advance on the traditional Continental Aesopic illustrations and the splendours of Hollar and Barlow.

Ogilby's Virgil (1654)

The Works of Publius Virgilius Maro, Translated, adorn'd and illustrated with Annotations, by John Ogilby, 'Printed by Thomas Warren for the Author, and are to be had at his House in Kings-head Court in Shoe-Lane. 1654' marks Ogilby's entry into publishing. A revision of his unillustrated 1649 translation, it is a grand folio with marginal commentaries, mainly second-hand. It is also Francis Cleyn's chief work as an illustrator. First come a haughty portrait of Ogilby engraved by William Faithorne after Peter Lely ('Lilly') and a facing frontispiece (362 × 251 mm.) in tribute to Virgil, designed by Cleyn and engraved by Pierre Lombart (1621?–1680). Another special plate (362 × 450 mm.) is a double-spread map of Italy and Greece by Hollar. There are a hundred and one large illustrations (c. 255 × 195 mm.), under each of which, on the same plate, is engraved in Latin the passage being illustrated and a dedication to a high-born subscriber together with his arms. Of these plates seventy-four carry Cleyn's name as designer, and Ludwig Richer signed one 'Inuen. fec'. Cleyn probably designed most, possibly all, of the remaining twenty-six on which the artist is not named, but it is impossible to tell.

Five hands etched and engraved the illustrations. Of the signed plates Hollar etched forty-two, Pierre Lombart engraved thirty-six, William Faithorne engraved two, and W. Carter etched one. In addition Richer initialed two others, 'R.f.' and 'L. R. f.', but it is not clear whether or not he designed only the one plate that he claimed as his own. Lombart seems to have engraved the majority of the unsigned plates. Carter, an imitator of Hollar and probably his pupil, also etched Cleyn's Five Senses series (1646). In the dedication Ogilby speaks of using the 'skill and industry of the most famous Artists, in their kinds, for the embellishing of the Work', an indication of Cleyn's reputation, no less than Hollar's and Lombart's. Hollar etched some of his own charming section initials and a number of pleasant putti and animal headings (46 × 188 mm.) drawn by Cleyn. (Carter initialled two of the headpieces.) With minor aberrations Ogilby used both frontispieces and all the illustrations from this edition in his Latin Virgil (1658), and later Tonson used them in the Dryden folio (1697) with Virgil and Apollo by Michael van der Gucht in place of Ogilby's portrait. Tonson

burnished out the lettering and arms in the panel at the bottom of each illustration and engraved a simple dedication to the new subscriber at '5 guineas a cut'.
The plates otherwise were untouched, except for a clumsy romanizing of Aeneas'
nose in each of eight plates (Tonson's feeble effort to flatter William III after
Dryden refused to dedicate the book to him). Spence in his *Anecdotes* (1820) says
that the success of the subscription was 'a good deal on account of the prints,
which were from Ogilby's plates touched up'. In 1709 Tonson entered the popular
market with an octavo third edition of Dryden's translation, the original Cleyn
designs being copied in reduced and uninspired form by van der Gucht.

In the 1654 Virgil Hollar provides a sidelight, as he does in later books, on the
production schedule of a book of this elaborateness by dating an occasional plate:
three 1652, six 1653, and one 1654. Two of the 1652 plates come in the book long
after four of the 1653 plates, and one of the 1653 plates comes four plates after the
1654 one. The distribution of assignments is so consistent though irregular that
it seems planned to avoid long sections of engraving changing abruptly to long
sections of etching. In any case Hollar began making plates two years before publication. Cleyn therefore probably began on the drawings soon after the Aesop
series in order to complete many, perhaps all, of them by 1652.

In the Virgil we have to come to a judgment about Cleyn's work when it is
interpreted by different hands and by both etching and engraving techniques.
Mindful of these hazards, we must still grant Cleyn credit for one of the impressive successes in English book illustration. Filling seventy-four, possibly even a
hundred, plates with complex designs of shepherds and poets amid the pastoral
scenes of the *Bucolics* and *Georgics* (fig. 35) and then of Aeneas in his travels and
battles is in itself impressive. An average of one of these stately illustrations every
six pages, crammed with heroic actors, mythological wonders, and seemingly
authentic backgrounds – as Hermes in the air visiting Aeneas as he supervises
the craftsmen building a palace at Carthage (fig. 36) – produces an almost syn-
chronic relationship of image to the opulent eventfulness of the narrative. The
elaborate plates do not achieve all of the pastoral charm and epic grandeur aimed
at, but they are effective illustrations of these classics because of the fidelity with
which the hundreds of figures, enlivened by Mannerist postures and strong
contrasts, re-enact the multitudinous incidents once minutely familiar to every
schoolboy.

35) CLEYN, from *The Works of Publius Virgilius Maro*, trans. Ogilby, 258 × 195 mm.

F. Cleyn inu. W. Hollar fecit

Ogilby's Iliad *and* Odyssey

From the Virgil Ogilby went back to Homer and published his folio *Iliad* (1660) and his folio *Odyssey* (1665). He presumably had his translation of *Homer His Iliads* completed by 1656, for one illustration is signed 'F. Clein inv. W. Hollar fecit 1656'. Hollar gives Cleyn credit for two other designs. In addition to the coat of arms of Charles II, to whom the work is dedicated, and an unsigned statue of Homer with a bee, Hollar etched only one other plate. Cleyn may have designed this one, too. Of the forty-nine illustrations only the first and last mention another artist. He is a follower of Rubens, Abraham van Diepenbeeck (1596–1675) of Antwerp, who may have visited England about 1657. Associated with him on the *Iliad* is the engraver Cornelis Caukercken (1626–1680).

The illness of Cleyn may have forced Ogilby to seek help on the *Iliad* even before Cleyn's death in 1658. Van Diepenbeeck drew a huge frontispiece (381 × 259 mm.) of a bust of Homer and a queen and warriors. The engraver is Pierre Lombart, who according to his custom adds 'Londini' after his name. Lombart signed only his own name to eight illustrations, and Caukercken signed only his to one. Since Cleyn and van Diepenbeeck compose similar designs, it is not possible to say how many of the forty-four unattributed illustrations each drew. Perhaps all are by van Diepenbeeck. For some reason Lombart also engraved another copy of the Lely portrait of Ogilby, hardly distinguishable from Faithorne's.

Van Diepenbeeck drew the designs for a great folio, *La Methode nouvelle . . . de dresser les Chevaux Traduite de l'Anglais de l'Auteur en François par son Commandement* (J. van Meurs, Antwerp, 1658) by William Cavendish, first Duke of Newcastle, cousin of William Cavendish, Earl of Devonshire. The author was then an exile training horses near Antwerp, but the backgrounds of the gigantic plates of horses going through their paces include a number of great houses, such as Bolsover, Bothel, and Ogle, which van Diepenbeeck might possibly have drawn in England. The backgrounds also include fields and some incidental hunting scenes of no special merit. Although the book is a foreign production, these English scenes, together with the main pictures of horses, to a small degree anticipate Barlow's English landscapes and sporting prints. Caukercken is one of the engravers, and Voersterman one of the etchers.

For *Homer His Odysses* (1665) Ogilby again called on Abraham van Diepenbeeck as his artist, presumably for all of the twenty-four full-page designs (*c.* 262 × 185 mm.), although his name is on only three. Cornelis Caukercken, P. Willems, I. Meyssens, A. Hertoch, and David Loggan shared the engraving. Only the last two seem to have been in England at the time. In addition to the Lely-Lombart portrait of Ogilby, there are also a van Diepenbeeck-Caukercken

36) CLEYN, from *The Works of Publius Virgilius Maro*, 254 × 190 mm.

frontispiece and a portrait of Prince James, Earl of Ormond, 'sculp et exc:' by Loggan. Since van Diepenbeeck is not even a resident alien, we need say only that these huge plates graphically depict for the first time in an English book immortal moments, such as those of Achilles dragging Hector's body around Troy and Odysseus discovering himself to Nausicaa, and they have an honourable place in Ogilby's effort to make plentiful illustration a significant part of the publication of literature in England. His success can be gauged by Spence's report that Ogilby's *Odyssey* was 'one of the first large poems that ever Mr. Pope read; and he still spoke of the pleasure it then gave him, with a sort of rapture . . . "It was that great edition with pictures. I was then about eight years old. This led me to Sandys' Ovid [with Cleyn's illustrations]."'

Except in the etched transcripts by Hollar, Francis Cleyn is not an appealing illustrator. Yet his years of working in England and his illustrations for Ovid's *Metamorphoses*, Ogilby's *Fables of Aesop Paraphras'd*, and Virgil's *Eclogues, Georgics*, and *Aeneid* entitle him to be remembered as the second important known book illustrator in England and a worthy forerunner of Hollar and Barlow.

CHAPTER V

The Minor Works of Barlow

THE MINOR WORKS for which Barlow provided illustrations or frontispieces came out at such irregular intervals throughout his career and are so miscellaneous that they tend to be lost in a chronological account. Therefore it seems advisable to gather them into one chapter and dispose of them before taking up major works by him and Hollar.

The Electra *Portrait of Princess Elizabeth* (*1649*)

The first etching and the first design for a book attributed to Barlow is unsigned, and no documentary evidence that he did it is available. It is an engaging portrait of the twelve- or thirteen-year old Princess Elizabeth Stuart within an ornate frame (fig. 37) (165 × 108 mm.). She was the second daughter and the third child of Charles I. The young girl is dressed in black, but a cupid, floating above her, withdraws a mourning veil from about her head, and two engraved couplets in a cartouche urge her to come forth from the 'Cypresse Bower' of grief. Against a grey background the insouciant cupid, the dark mourning apparel, and the white skin create lively etched line and tonal effects, an innovative relief from the stiff engraved portraits of Elizabethan and Stuart frontispieces. It is unpretentious, yet it is an event in the history of English etching and book illustration. I do not find a record of an earlier published etching by an English-born artist. In England only Hollar had published etched portraits, notably his copies of Van Dyck's paintings of the royal family, including those of Elizabeth's older sister Mary as the child bride of Prince William of Orange. They surpass this *Electra* frontispiece in skill though not in charm. Before we can give young Barlow credit for it, therefore, we must examine the circumstances of its publication, as well as its style, with some care.

The portrait occurs as the frontispiece to a 1649 translation of Sophocles' *Electra* by 'C.W.' (Christopher Wase, 1625 ?–1690). Wase entered King's College, Cambridge, in 1645 and graduated in classics in 1648. His *Electra* is perhaps the

37) BARLOW, from Sophocles: *Electra*, trans. Wase, 165 × 108 mm.

earliest English edition of a play by Sophocles. The title-page says the book was printed 'At the Hague, for Sam. Brown'. The royalist bookseller-printer was indeed in business at The Hague from 1643 to 1660, but in the *Electra* he serves as a red-herring, as he did in relation to various editions of the *Eikon Basilike* and *Reliquiae Sacrae Carolinae*, issued about the same time. A comparison of the *Electra* with these deceptive editions and with books actually published by Brown at The Hague leaves no doubt that it was also printed in England, presumably in London. The type and the setting are so like those of Denny's *Pelecanicidium*, to be discussed next, that the two books may well have come from the same printing-shop.

One imagines that Wase in Cambridge had the translation and scholarly notes well in hand when the execution of Charles I on 30 January 1649, the day after his agonizing last interview with the precocious Elizabeth and her eight-year old brother Henry, suggested to Wase the aptness of casting her in the role of Electra and dedicating the book to her as a means of showing his loyalty to the Stuarts and courting future royal favour. As a hostage of Parliament in the custody of the Earl of Northumberland Elizabeth was in England; the rest of the royal family except young Henry were abroad. The introductory matter consists of a flattering dedication to the Princess and four complimentary poems addressed to Wase. Then he added an Epilogue 'Shewing the Parallel between the theme of the *Electra* and the future of the Stuarts in two Poems, the Return and the Restauration'. Apparently as an afterthought it was deemed politic to increase the recognition of Elizabeth's oldest brother Charles, the Orestes of the 'parallel' and now Charles II to the Cavaliers, by introducing a plain little oval engraved portrait of him. He is identified only by 'IERSEY' on a ribbon in the print and 'Aetatis suae 19' beneath it. Since Charles arrived on the island of Jersey in September 1649, the book came out later in the year. (George Thomason bought his copy on 5 April [1650].) It seems reasonable to think that Wase in Cambridge turned for publication to a London bookseller and that he in turn hired a London artist to prepare a frontispiece. In fact, the artist was almost certainly in England because the portrait seems copied from Lely's full-length painting of Elizabeth and her brothers James and Henry, now at Petworth, Sussex, done in 1646/7. The *Electra* copyist used etching, a relatively uncommon technique in England until the nineteenth century, but he discreetly refrained from signing the plate. Hollar and Gaywood have been suggested as this etcher. Hollar could hardly have done it. He went to Antwerp before Lely painted the royal children, then in England.

In 1649 Hollar etched a copy of William Marshall's engraved frontispiece for one of the editions of the *Eikon Basilike* that Samuel Brown was licensed to print and sell at The Hague with a formal statement to that effect on the title-page. The

Defence de la Religion Reformée et de la Monarchie et Eglise Anglicane (1650) is another example of one of the books actually published by Brown at The Hague. On the title-page is the statement 'Imprimé a la Hay. L'An Second après le Martyre de Charles I . . . Chez Samuel Broun Libraire Anglois. 1650'. Furthermore it contains an unidealized etched portrait (105 × 83 mm.) of the twenty-year old 'Carolus II' (fig. 38). If by any chance Hollar had etched the *Electra* portrait of Elizabeth, and a comparison shows that Hollar's style is unmistakably different, it seems likely that he would have done this one of Charles at the same time. On the death of the Princess Elizabeth at Carisbrooke Castle, Isle of Wight, in 1650, he did etch and date a nearly facsimile copy of the *Electra* plate without the cupid or the veil. A cropped example of this print is at the British Museum. As for Gaywood, at his limited best as a portrait etcher, as in the frontispiece of Clarke's *Mirror for Saints and Sinners* (1657), he assiduously imitates Hollar. Barlow is the logical candidate.

38) HOLLAR, from Anon: *Le Defence de la Religion Reformée*, 105 × 83 mm.

In 1649 Barlow was about twenty-three; yet by 1650 he had satisfied the requirements for membership in the Painter-Stainers Company, and thus he had had
time to become proficient in etching. There is no reason to doubt that he was
in England in 1649 and could have had access to the Lely painting. The most
convincing reason to believe that Barlow is the artist, however, is the close
resemblance between the *Electra* frontispiece and the etched plates in Barlow's
immediately subsequent *Pelecanicidium* and *Theophila* illustrations and several heads
in the later *Aesop's Fables*. In general they have in common a distinctive freedom
of technique and naturalism of effects. Specifically, the treatment of the cupid
and the Princess is closely similar to that of the angels and 'Man' in the illustration for Canto III of *Theophila*. And the sly shaping of the acanthus leaves at the
base of the *Electra* border into the semblance of the top of an owl's face is the sort
of whimsy we might expect from Barlow.

We can accept without further hesitation that the *Electra* Princess Elizabeth
frontispiece is by Francis Barlow and a significant, if modest, first step in his
career as an illustrator. True, as was customary and inescapable, he borrowed the
features. But the airy cupid pulling aside the veil signals the arrival of the first
identifiable major native English talent to interpret a text in visual terms that have
their own grace.

The Pelecanicidium *Signed Plates*

'F. Barlow fecit' on all of the etched designs in Sir William Denny's mixture of
verse and prose quaintly entitled *Pelecanicidium: or the Christian Adviser against Self-
Murder* (1653) makes these plates a dependable referent for Barlow's etching
technique. These plates confirm beyond any doubt that Barlow is the etcher of at
least ten of the unsigned *Theophila* plates. They are second only to those plates as
evidence of Barlow's early competence as an etcher and as an imaginative illustrator. The probable date of issue of *Pelecanicidium* was early in 1653 (NS), for it
was entered to Thomas Hucklescott in the Stationers Register on 17 December
1652, and in accordance with his custom George Thomason, assembler of the
great collection of tracts at the British Library, inscribed on his copy (E.1233) the
date that he came into possession of it – 27 February 1652 (OS).

Above Denny's arms in the frontispiece plate (160 × 101 mm.) is a decorative
arrangement of a pelican with her wings half spread and her neck curved into a
full circle in order to force from her own breast sustenance for four hungry
young ones. On a tree at the left a python-like snake symbolizes evil; on one at
the right, a dove, goodness. The design as a whole is not attractive, but it shows
what authority and ingenuity Barlow brought to the drawing of natural creatures.

39) BARLOW, from Denny: *Pelicanicidium*, 124 × 88 mm.

The frontispiece to Book I, 'The Christian Adviser Against Self-Homicide, or Self-Murder' (fig. 39) (124 × 88 mm.), features a young woman like Theophila pressing toward a magnificent eagle with the Bible in his talons. Uncrowded, the illustration also includes a cat snoozing, a tiger springing, atop a cliff an angel restraining a would-be suicide, and a devil leering above a gallows. Beneath the design are four lines of verse engraved in an additional 15 mm. space on the same plate.

In the frontispiece for the second book (repeated for the third), 'A Guide to the Land of the Living':

Wise Traveller through Wildernesse does lead
The Christian Pilgrim, teaching where to tread;
From Feind in World's Way Foes he warnes his Freind.
Through deepe, up Steepe, shewes Heavn's his Journeys end.

The Traveller is realistically presented in the elegant but dignified dark clothes of a contemporary gentleman. He leads by the hand the Christian in contrasting white pilgrim habit and gestures upward to the celestial city (also seen in Canto V of *Theophila*), which is their goal. They walk on a narrow upward-twisting path with an abyss on both sides, and near their feet lurk a hellish dragon and venomous snakes. The design owes something to the emblem books, and *Pilgrim's Progress* may owe something in turn to it. Both the radiant celestial city and the narrow horizontal shading on the ruffled trousers show the close relation of this plate and the next to last of the *Theophila* series. Denny's concepts are much simpler to visualize than Benlowes', and Barlow needed no aid from the author to invent his designs. His stature as an interpretive illustrator, however, is measured by what he does here, as in *Theophila*, to give credibility, largeness, and dignity to thoughts merely indicated in verse.

Other Frontispieces and Title-pages

Among Barlow's minor works several unpretentious frontispiece and title-page designs might be mentioned together. The design (112×63 mm.) for John Brown's pocket *Description and Use of the Carpenters-Rule* (1656) shows a well-dressed master carpenter standing before an open doorway with a swag above it. He holds the emblems of his trade, a right angle in one hand and dividers in the other. Three geometric shapes for instruction stand about. The plate is etched and signed 'R. Gaywood fecit', but the original drawing at the British Museum (C-M&H, pl. 53[a]) is without doubt by Barlow.

We have already noted that at Christmas 1656 Barlow and Gaywood presented John Evelyn with an etched copy of one of Titian's paintings of Venus and an organist – the one with a dark organist and a formal garden outside. The painting is now in the Prado, having once belonged to Charles I. It was acquired by Charles IV of Spain during the sale of Charles I's great collection between 1650 and 1653. Barlow must therefore have made his drawing some years before 1656. If he had made the drawing while Charles I was still in Whitehall, he must have secured permission to copy it from the Lord Chamberlain, probably through

Abraham van der Doort, keeper of the King's collection. The print is a considerable effort (262 × 384 mm.). Barlow ends the flattering engraved Latin dedication 'Franciscus Barlous Pingendi benevolus dedicavit'. He may have thought that his role was not clear because Gaywood had signed the plate ambiguously 'R. Gaywood fecit aqua forti Londini 1656'. In the obsequious accompanying note Barlow says that he let 'Mr Gaywood my friend' sign the plate because it might be to his advantage to do so. He explains carefully, however, that he himself made the drawing from the original painting, drew it on the plate, and finished (i.e., etched) the heads of both figures, hands and feet, the dog that Venus toys with, and the landscape. After the rebuff from Evelyn, Barlow may have removed the dedication and pulled a number of impressions. In 1675 the print dealer Arthur Tooker advertised a print by Gaywood under the title 'Titian and His Mistress', which is probably this one. It seems the only instance where Barlow engaged in so elaborate an effort in reproducing another artist's painting. The working relationship with Richard Gaywood (c. 1630?–1680) lasted at least fifteen years, perhaps longer. Gaywood seems to have been an industrious but mechanical reproductive etcher who often signed only his name to plates but attempted only modest designs of his own. He cannot be considered a book illustrator. On one of Barlow's bird plates he signed 'R. Gaywood fecit & Excudit', but it is not clear what he meant by that.

Gaywood etched and engraved a portrait and two title-pages (235 × 147 mm.) for Samuel Clarke's *A Mirror or Looking Glass for Saints and Siners* [sic] (1656) and *A Geographicall Description of all the Countries in the knowne World,* which were issued by Thomas Newbery as one volume (1657). The oval portrait (145 × 109 mm.) of the industrious minister of St. Bennet Fink, who signed his dedications cosily 'From my study in Thridneedle street', is a good imitation of Hollar's technique by his pupil Gaywood. It is dated 1654. He also signed both title-pages 'R. Gaywood fecit', but Barlow drew the designs, as can be seen by comparing the original drawing of the *Geographicall Description* plate (c-m&h, pl. 54).

The two title-pages have a uniform plan: engraved text surrounded by illustrative panels. In the *Mirror* the top panel shows a Papist dismayed at what he sees in a mirror, while a Protestant remains serene. The bottom panel of Nineveh and Jerusalem contains small figures of a bear, a lion, and several other animals. The bottom panel of the *Geographicall Description* contains larger figures of an elephant and a rhinoceros, and the side panels (L) a horse and a lion and (R) an elephant and a camel. All of these animals resemble Barlow's as etched by Gaywood in Ogilby's *Aesopics* and *Androcleus*, especially the lion. The thought of featuring animals in the second title-page instead of other aspects of geography would occur to Barlow. These Barlow designs for Clarke's title-pages are noteworthy in only one respect: they represent a rejection of baroque formalism in favour of English naturalism.

The frontispiece of the fifth edition of North's translation of Plutarch's *Lives* (Abraham Miller, 1657) has only the explicit signature 'Francis Barlow Inventer'. The large plate (290 × 189 mm.) is engraved, with some of the finer detail etched. Although Gaywood liked to sign his own name and 'fecit', probably he prepared the plate after Barlow's design. The concept is traditional but not mechanically so. An engraved bust of Plutarch, within the border of an emblematic circular snake biting its own tail, is flanked by clumsy men in armour representing 'A Grecian' and 'A Roman'. Beneath in small compartments are etched two walled cities, 'Athens' and 'Rome', and a sea battle and a land battle. The cities are almost identical with those in the Nineveh and Jerusalem panel in Clarke's *Mirror*. Above, and mostly etched in the Hollar manner, Fame as an angel with many small eyes and ears dotting her outspread wings holds a laurel wreath over the heads of each of the two warriors. In a cartouche is the bookseller Lee's advertisement, dated 1656. A certain grace in the angel suggests that in abler hands Barlow's 'invention' would have been much more impressive and appealing.

One of the best of the Barlow-Gaywood frontispieces is the signed eight-compartment one in the folio *Annals of the Old and New Testament: with Synchronismus of Heathen Story to the Destruction of Hierusalem by the Romanes* (1658) by James Us[s]her, Abp. of Armagh *in absentia*. It was printed by E. Tyler for J. Crook and G. Bedell and on the printed title-page changes its name to *The Annals of the World*. The scholarly Usher, who tried to persuade Charles I not to abandon Strafford, is now remembered chiefly because in the Latin first edition of this work he dated Creation *c.* 4000 B.C. Barlow's large design (300 × 185 mm.) contains an Adam and Eve surrounded by animals in the Garden in the centre at the top and a Last Supper at the bottom, Solomon and Nebuchadnezzar in the top corners and Cyrus and Vespazian in the bottom corners, and on the sides two temples of Jerusalem before and after destruction by the Romans.

The strength and weakness of the Barlow-Gaywood team are nowhere more obvious than in the large frontispiece (fig. 40) (237 × 132 mm.) for the Historiographer–Royal James Howell's philosophical bestiary, Θηρολογια, or *The Queen Of the Inchanted Iland* [*The Parly of Beasts, or Morphandra*] (1660). It is an anticipation of their later fable work together. Princess Morphandra, who can change men to animals and animals to men, and Prince Pererus, her attendant, stand on a cloud in the upper half of the design. Gaywood has made a hash of engraving the Roman figures, though carefully marked M and P. But below in a half-circle looking up are a wolf, an ass, an ape, a goose, a goat, a fox, a boar, a deer, and an otter. (The point of view is a gratuitously difficult one.) There is also a hive of bees but no mule – Barlow doubtless thought the ass would be enough. These animals are a revelation, in book form at least, of the arrival of the first native-born artist who was able to draw animals in a way both realistic and attractive. And Gaywood seems to have been aware that the occasion should be more accurately recorded than some of the others, for he signs the plate 'F. Barlowe Inu: R Gaywood fecit'. Thus this plate serves as one basis for identifying their work later, especially the unsigned plates in Ogilby's *Aesopics* and *Androcleus* (1668). The important point about the plate otherwise is its testimony as to how far the scientific spirit had penetrated Barlow's animal drawings a century before George Stubbs published his *Anatomy of the Horse*.

Both conscientious and appealing is Barlow's frontispiece (80 × 133 mm.) for John Playford's little *Musick's Delight on the Cithren* (1666), a manual of instruction for playing the instrument, together with some music to play (fig. 41). (A cithern or cittern is a guitar with wire strings.) As a sign of the influx of foreigners in the arts after the Restoration, Playford says scornfully that even a city tap-wife is 'ambitious to have her daughter taught by Monsieur La Novo Kickshawibus on the Gittar'. Barlow draws a seated Cavalier plucking a cithern with the book open on a table. On the wall hang a mandolin, a bass viol, and a kit. Presumably

41) BARLOW, from Playford: *Musicks' Delight on the Cithren*, 80 × 133 mm.

40) BARLOW, from Howell: Θηρολοιγα, *or The Queen of the Inchanted Island*, 237 × 132 mm.

M

P

the scene is meant to represent Playford's shop 'in the Temple'. Once more Gaywood signs only his own name to his drily etched and engraved plate, but the original drawing at the British Museum (C-M&H, pl. 53ᵇ) is manifestly by Barlow. Modest as the design is, it has a homely authenticity.

A. F. Johnson in his *Catalogue of Engraved and Etched Title-Pages* (1934) ascribed the title-page (and presumably the forty-five illustrations by the same hand) of Philip Ayres' *Emblemata Amatoria* (1683) to Barlow. The title-page only has an ornamental monogram that could be I.B. or possibly I.R. but not F.B. Furthermore, Barlow never used a monogram. H. Thomas in *The Library* (January 1910) suggested that it is I.B. for Isaac Beckett. It is impossible to imagine Barlow in 1683 copying and etching from the 1608 Antwerp edition these cupids and miserable animals.

Two Illustrations for Stapylton's Juvenal

In 1660, the year of the Restoration and the inflow of Dutch artists and craftsmen that Charles II had learned to admire while abroad, R. Hodgkinson printed Sir Robert Stapylton's translation, *Mores Hominum, The Manners of Men Described in Sixteen Satyrs by Juvenal* with illustrations by Danckerts, Streater, Barlow, and Hollar. Since Hollar etched and engraved all of the plates for the illustrations, and Barlow drew only two designs, we shall look at the book as a whole when we review Hollar's work in illustrated books.

Barlow's two signed plates, uniform with the rest, are unusually large. The first (284 × 200 mm.), illustrating the satire of the proconsul Marcus Aurelius Marius, is a circular composition of the boon companions of a young aristocrat seated about a round table in a drinking bout. Nothing about the treatment suggests Barlow, but there are similar round-table scenes in *Androcleus* and the Life of Aesop. The thief, hangman, coffin-maker, and other uncouth fellows make the satire palpable as they gesture drunkenly in contrast to the reclining nobleman. The repetition several times of the same-shaped wine pitchers adds an elegant touch. The bending figure of the host, cook Syrophaenix, serving makes a pleasant counter rhythm in the circle.

The second design (fig. 42) (278 × 197 mm.) seems more congenial for Barlow because Satire XI permits a more attractive scene – Juvenal himself entertaining a friend on plain fare to accompany a feast of poetry. Juvenal, unfortunately looking dour, sits on one side of an open horseshoe table, his friend on the other. On the table is a sparse assortment of food including chicken, asparagus, and eggs. The two small boys who approach Juvenal with baskets of grapes and two others who wait beside the unserved wine, one holding a copy of Homer, the

42) BARLOW, from *Mores Hominum, The Manners of Men Described in Sixteen Satyrs by Juvenal*, trans. Stapylton, 278 × 197 mm.

Barlow inv: Hollar fec: 1667

other of Virgil, are unaffectedly charming, something quite new in English illustration. On the spacious checker-board tile floor are the signatures 'Barlow inv.' and 'W. Hollar fec. 1659'.

Bird and Animal Manuals

Barlow drew several different series of birds and animals, but they cannot be discussed individually here because, although issued in book form, they are collections of prints without text, not illustrated books. He was following a long established custom of providing manuals for apprentice artists and artisans in related fields, such as goldsmiths, sculptors, embroiderers, ceramists, and 'such as practice Drawing, Graveing, Armes Painting, Chaseing', who might not have the opportunity to sketch from life an eagle or a rhinoceros, not to mention basilisks, griffins, phoenixes, or unicorns, or even be clever at drawing hens, cows and hoopoes. Collections of flowers, fruits, insects, and formal motifs were also common. Gheeraerts, Jacques le Moyne, Crispin van de Passe, and John Payne had prepared manuals that Barlow would have known, and it was natural for him to apply his talent for drawing birds and animals to similar collections. In one of his series he acknowledges that one of his designs is copied after Frans Snyders, the Antwerp painter of animals and hunting scenes, whose work must have appealed to him immensely.

Barlow's prints exist in confusing mixtures of separate proofs and desecrated pages as well as in bound assortments and in scattered collections. It therefore would be a scholarly, useful, and pleasant exercise for someone to catalogue the editions of new Barlow designs, reprints, and copies, together with extant drawings. The earliest dated series seems one indicated by a plate (126 × 181 mm.) of an eagle, with other birds in the four corners, on which is engraved 'Fran: Barlow inu: W. Hollar fecit Londini 1654 P.S. [Peter Stent] exc.' (Parthey 2135). The next dated series seems one published by William Faithorne: *Diversae Avium Species studiosissime ad vitam delineatae Per Fra: Barlow insignissimī: Anglum Pictorem – Gulielm: Faithorne excudit 1658*. The title is engraved on the skin of a deer held in the beaks of two eagles with wings spread. This handsome etched design is signed 'F. Barlow Inuen: R Gaywood fecit'.

But Barlow etched at least one series, and perhaps only one, himself, probably in the 1650s, possibly even earlier than 1654. A small incomplete series (91 × 128 mm.) of a dozen etchings occurs loose in a mixed collection of proofs in the British Museum under the grand title *Multae et diversae Avium Species Multifarijs Formis & Pernaturalebus Figuris per Franciscum Barlovium Anglum Artis Pingendi celeberremae Philomusum Indigenam Londinensem*. The set appears with the same title-

43) BARLOW, *proof title-page*, 91 × 128 mm.

plate but 'with new additions' in an edition published by John Overton (1671). The technique is refined and resembles Hollar's – in fact Parthey assigns the series to Hollar. But the only signatures are the initials FB backwards on stones in two prints and 'F Barlow invent' on a stone in the 'Lapwinks' plate. The lack of a Hollar (or Gaywood) signature, the forgetting to reverse the fancy initials (a youthful affectation), the name on the stone (an early imitative mannerism), spellings like 'Pegions', 'Feasonts', and 'Wild Dookes', all point to Barlow alone. But the most convincing evidence (accepted by Mr. Paul Hulton) that both drawings and etchings are by Barlow himself is the stunning veracity of the drama of the snakes making a kill in the lower corners of the title plate (fig. 43).

Otherwise Barlow's manuals were etched and engraved by Hollar, Gaywood, Place, Griffier, Vaughan, Kip, and others for series of different sizes. Some of the original plates were copied and reissued as late as *Divers Species of Birds & Drawn after the Life in their Natural Altitudes* [*sic*] *by Francis Barlow* (Laurie & Whittle, 1799). On 9 January 1685/6 in a letter to the etcher Francis Place, in

Yorkshire, the print publisher Pierce Tempest, a fellow Yorkshireman, gives a glimpse of Barlow and seventeenth-century print-selling, timeless in its ordinariness. He complains about Place's slowness. 'Barlow is now beginning with some of the large designes of birds. I will have a plate ready Against you come up [to London] ... remember to bring Barlows 6 drawings with you I beleeve we may have them Inlarged to the bigger size ... hopeing you have had a merry Xmas for my part I have left off Wine and strong drink to a Plate of New Milk at night.'

Barlow was one of the artists who made drawings of plants for Robert Morison's *Plantarum Historiae Universales Oxoniensis pars secunda seu Herbarum Distributio Nova. Oxon.* (1680–1699). (Part one was not published.) They are mere outlines, drawn only for accuracy, and arranged in three or more rows on a page. Four pages are signed 'Fr. Barlow delin.', three of them engraved by David Loggan, pupil of Hollar and recorder of seventeenth-century Oxford. Many pages are unsigned or signed only by the engraver, so that Barlow may have been responsible for more than four pages. These prosaic drawings tell us nothing except that Barlow and Loggan were not too proud or affluent to take on so minor an assignment at this time and that sometimes their work was far below their usual standard.

Books of Sports

In 1671, again with Hollar as his etcher and John Overton as his printer, Barlow illustrated and published *Seuerall Wayes of Hunting, Hawking, & Fishing according to the English Manner* for the benefit of foreign sportsmen. It is not a work of literature, but it is an important publication in the history of British sports. It is literary to the extent that the brief and humble text, presumably by Barlow, takes the form of two explanatory couplets engraved on each of nine plates (*c.* 151 × 217 mm.). The format is a long rectangle because the etchings are anecdotal scenes. Barlow is in his element. He has plenty of action by country gentlemen, amply supported by attendants with poles and eager hounds, as they hunt hare (fig. 44, the original drawing in the Ashmolean Museum), stag, fox, conies [rabbits], and otter. (1671 is the year of the law barring freeholders of under £100 from killing game on their own land, much to the advantage of the squires.) Three plates show the differences in hawking for partridge, hern, and pheasant, and one plate makes clear that river fishing can be much more elaborate than it seems in the idyllic scene of the single fisherman with a pole in Barlow's Aesop.

The title-page says 'Etched by W. Hollar', but he completed and signed only two plates. He apparently etched the backgrounds of most of the rest, but Gaywood etched and engraved the figures, except for those in 'Cony Catching'. They

44) BARLOW, drawing for *Severall Ways of Hunting, Hawking and Fishing*, 151 × 217 mm.

were engraved by one of the anonymous hands who executed Barlow's *Aesopics* designs. On the two signed plates Hollar seems to have lost his fastidious touch, possibly because of his poor sight or other physical failing. Yet the book is one of the first of the long line of British illustrated sporting books. Wynkyn de Worde's *Boke of Hawkynge and Huntynge*, 1496, is the first (fig. 10), and two by George Turbervile, 1575, are the first realistic ones (fig. 16). It is also one of the first of English illustrated books to use the English countryside in an intimate way that will become the idiom of countless later books.

Barlow is apparently the chief illustrator of *The Gentleman's Recreation* (1686) by Richard Blome. It is a folio of universal knowledge in two parts, including treatises on horsemanship, hawking, hunting, fowling, fishing, agriculture, and cockfighting, printed for Blome by S. Roycroft. According to the *Dictionary of National Biography* Blome was considered 'an impudent person' who by means of 'progging tricks' induced hacks to write for him and cozened noblemen to subscribe to a dozen or more volumes of heraldry and geography. The printed titlepage says that the book is 'illustrated with about an Hundred Ornamental and Useful Sculptures, Engraven in Copper'.

The second part of *The Gentleman's Recreation* contains thirty-eight full-page illustrations and six oval plates with text. Two of the illustrations are signed 'F. Barlow delin.' The first is for 'Manning Hawks' (293 × 210 mm. plus a 55 mm. engraved dedication at the bottom). It is engraved by Arthur Soly, who signs several of the plates and seems to have done many of the unsigned ones. He dates one 1683 and another 1684. He is a poor engraver, but under his butcher's hand we can still trace a characteristic Barlow design. In the foreground of 'Manning Hawks' a falconer and his dogs encircle a hawk pinnning a bird to the ground; in the middle ground hunters loose a hawk after a bird. The original drawing is in the Witt Collection at the Courtauld Institute Gallery.

The second signed illustration (270 × 193 mm. plus a 38 mm. dedication) is signed 'Ni.Yeates Sculp.' (fig. 45). It is the most attractive plate in the book. Eight men spear otters, while hounds stand barking on the edge of two streams. Yeates' etching of Barlow's dogs, otters, pollarded trees, and a heron and two ducks flying is not painfully inferior to that by Barlow and Hollar. Yeates signs another plate, 'The Setting Dogg & Partridge'. It is clearly after Barlow, but it is not quite so interesting as the otter design. Thirteen other designs seem almost certainly to be by Barlow's hand. Of the illustrations in the second book, therefore, two plates are signed by Barlow, thirteen carry evidence of his authorship, and he might have done some of twelve others. Most of Barlow's designs have been wretchedly served by inexpert engravers, but in the two plates by Yeates and in the Witt drawing we have the proof that the original drawings for *The Gentle-*

45) BARLOW, from Blome: *The Gentleman's Recreation*, 279 × 193 mm.

HUNTING ỹ OTTER

F.Barlo delin.

N.Yeator Sculp.

man's Recreation must have been Barlow at his best. Even in their denatured state Barlow's series in their lively compositions and their celebration of country sporting life and the community of animals and men are an important extension of Barlow's *Hunting, Hawking, and Fishing* plates.

Of interest to connoisseurs of sporting and topical prints is Barlow's etching (300 × 507 mm.) of 'The Last Horse Race' because it is the first known English print of a horse race (fig. 46). The full inscribed title reads 'August 24, 1684 The last Horse Race Run before Charles the Second of Blessed Memory by Dorsett [Datchett] Ferry near Windsor Castle', but the plate was 'Drawn from the Place and Design'd by Francis Barlow 1687'. The figures, including the horses, are small and wooden, but the scene is recorded with the eye of an illustrator.

Guide Books

The friendly trio of John Ogilby, Barlow, and Hollar that came together in 1668 for Ogilby's *Aesopics* joined forces again in 1675 for Volume I of Cosmographer Ogilby's *Britannia*, one of the first road guides to England and Wales. Barlow drew and Hollar etched (the plate is signed) the title-page (fig. 47) (368 × 221 mm.). Barlow cannot be merely decorative: he penetrates the situation and turns the bare factual general into the human anecdotal particular. Thus what might have been only dissociated elements bordering a central printed title becomes a pleasant, almost garrulous English scene. Two riders issue from a fortified city gate above which flies the royal ensign. In the foreground are men studying road-maps, clearly with differing opinions then, as today, about the best way to reach Pembroke or Peterborough. This is one of the most interesting of English title-pages, but again, except for the winsome cherubs, the full charm of Barlow eludes the aging Hollar.

Ogilby's folio *Itinerarium Angliae: or, A Book of Roads* (1675) has the distinction of changing the English mile from 2428 yards to the statute mile of 1760 yards. 'Printed by the Author at his House in White-Fryers', it provides maps for the principal roads of England and Wales, 'actually admeasured and delineated in a century of whole-sheet copper-sculps' (323 × 457 mm.). Each sheet ingeniously shows a stretch of road engraved on six folds of a continuous ribbon. In the middle of each of the one hundred sheets is an engraved three-sided cartouche for the name of the region. Twenty-two of the cartouches also contain figure and animal designs that clearly show Barlow's hand. Of these, ten hunting and pastoral scenes appear to be etched by Nicholas Yeates.

Only one of the forty-eight illustrations of tombs in Francis Sandford's

46) BARLOW, *The Last Horse Race*, 300 × 507 mm.

The Road from
LONDON TO BARWICK
Tottenham high Crosse

MIDDLESEX

LONDON

WESTMOR
LAND
YORK
LANCASHIRE
LINCOLN
SHIRE

BRITANNIA
VOL. I
or an
Illustration
of ye Kingdom of
ENGLAND
and dominon of WALES
By a
Geographical & Historical
Description
of the Principal
ROADS.

Fran. Barlow invt.   W. Hollar fecit

Genealogical History of the Kings of England ('Tho. Newcomb in the Savoy for the Author', 1677) is signed 'F. Barlow Delin. R. Gaywood fecit', but some of the other nine signed by Gaywood and a few of those not signed at all might have been drawn by Barlow. Only Barlow could have drawn the ingratiating fawn at the feet of the effigy of a princess on page 320. Most of the plates are drawn and etched by Hollar. The one Barlow-signed plate is a massive affair of two towers, on which stand several figures, supporting a grill enclosing the tomb of William, Baron Russell, the first Baron Thornhaugh (1558?–1613). Our chief reaction to this design is one of mild astonishment that Barlow could discipline himself to make so elaborately finicky a drawing.

47) BARLOW, from Ogilby: *Brittania*, 368 × 221 mm.

CHAPTER VI

Barlow's Illustrations of
Theophila
by Edward Benlowes (1652)

THE FIRST INTERPRETIVE ILLUSTRATIONS by Francis Barlow are a remark-able series in Edward Benlowes' *Theophila* (1652), a 268-page religious poem in English and Latin printed by R. N. [Roger Norton] and sold by Henry Seile and Humphrey Moseley. The peculiar circumstances of the publication of the poem have to be reviewed at some length before Barlow's work can be isolated and appreciated. Benlowes (1602–1676) was a pious, rhapsodic, generous, gullible, fussy bachelor. With good reason the anagram 'Benevolus' was applied to him in flattering verse. Until his fortune ran out and litigation bedevilled him, he played the role of man of letters and patron to several authors including Phineas Fletcher and Francis Quarles. After a term in debtors' prison, Oxford, *c.* 1667, he spent his last years among the riches of the Bodleian, but he died of cold and want. He is now remembered chiefly because Pope made fun of him in *The Dunciad*: 'Benlowes, propitious still to blockheads'.

Benlowes, born a Catholic, turned Anglican in his youth and became anti-Catholic and anti-Puritan. He lived at Brent Hall, Finchingfield, in Parliamen-tarian Essex. Though he took up arms briefly for King Charles I, he was on good terms with individual men of opposing religious and political beliefs. Among his friends who wrote commendatory verse in or about *Theophila* were Sir William Denny, Thomas Philipott, and James Howell, three writers also associated with Barlow. As he had in Ogilby's *Aesop Paraphras'd*, Sir William Davenant, the royalist playwright, gave his address and the date: 'Tower, May 13th 1652'. This device for making his plight known may have helped secure his release, perhaps through Milton's intercession.

Theophila, or Love's-Sacrifice. A Divine Poem (the canto running-heads for the essential poem all read 'Theophila's Love-Sacrifice') is a confused religious work planned in eight cantos and then extended to thirteen. Much of it is in Latin and written in stumbling triple-rime, 5-4-6-beat numbered stanzas clotted with meta-physical similes, often violent, fantastic, ludicrous, and now and then fresh and luminous as in the verse of mystics like Crashaw. 'Theophila, or Divine Love [the

Soul], ascends to her Belov'd Christ', Benlowes explains. Harold Jenkins in his admirable scholarly study of Benlowes says succinctly that *Theophila* 'moves from ecstasy to ecstasy without coherence of incident'. In spite of its Anglicanism it reveals the prejudices of a Puritan and the raptures of a Counter-Reformation Catholic, and it probably contains more exclamation marks than any other poem in the language.

The Miscellaneous Designs

Jenkins has gone to a great deal of trouble to unravel the facts about the printing of *Theophila*, but some of the facts about the illustrations remain unclear. Apparently Roger Norton printed the text, and Seile and Moseley acted only as booksellers, while Benlowes planned and supervised the production, as is indicated by the idiosyncratic use of italics and upper-case type. Not only had Benlowes developed an interest in printing, engraving, and emblem books during a tour of the Continent; he had brought back with him John Schoren a Brussels printer, and installed him at Brent Hall with a 'rolling-press', the kind necessary for printing intaglio engravings and etchings. Extant copies of *Theophila* vary so much from one another that it seems few were sold and that Benlowes took the plates and a stock of sheets to Finchingfield and made up individual presentation copies according to his notion of suitability to recipients. Some of the prints found in some copies, however, are later insertions without any significance as illustrations.

A 'perfect' copy of *Theophila* is said to have twenty-five illustrations. This is something of a myth. Among them are nine extremely miscellaneous, mostly second-hand designs that seem to have been part of the plan of the book at the time of printing. They seem intended to be illustrations, but they cannot be taken seriously as interpretations of the text. In what seems their normal order of occurrence these designs are the following: a lady representing Winter from Hollar's small third set of Four-Seasons prints issued by Peter Stent (1644) (Parthey 617); a huge woodcut of Adam and Eve in the Garden from the 'Bishops' Bible' (Christopher Barker, 1584); an unsigned engraving of 'Astronomy' from Francis Cleyn's series of prints, 'Septem Liberales Artes' (1645); an ugly small plate engraved by William Marshall as a title-page for Benlowes' unpublished *Ludus Literarius Christianus* but borrowed from Marshall's design for Benlowes' *Quarlëis*; 'Summer', another lady from Hollar's 1644 Seasons (Parthey 615); two crude little engravings by Peregrine Lovell of a gallant and a toper (the right and left halves, respectively, of one plate cut in two); what looks like a discarded half-title for *Theophila* engraved by Pierre Lombart for a smaller format; and an early woodcut of Queen Elizabeth praying, the frontispiece from *The Book of*

Christian Prayers (Day, 1569). The woodcuts and some of the engravings were probably acquired by Norton during the family dispute with Robert Barker over the Royal Printing House, Blackfriars. These miscellaneous cuts and a few non-figurative plates contribute nothing to the book but confusion, and they have nothing to do with Barlow.

Only Barlow's series of ten etchings can be considered serious illustrations of the poem. Strangely, young Barlow did not sign any of the *Theophila* plates, and Benlowes makes no reference to him. But Vertue's testimony, two original drawings, and ample comparative evidence leave no question that he did design and etch this series. In addition, a portrait of the poet and a large design of Theophila vanquishing a dragon have also been attributed to Barlow.

Benlowes' Portrait and Theophila Triumphant

Of immediate interest are these two companion pieces, a handsome portrait of Benlowes (fig. 48) (281 × 181 mm.) and, usually facing Canto IX, a companion piece by the same hand, Theophila triumphing over evil (fig. 49) (272 × 175 mm.). In the second plate Theophila stands with one foot on a vanquished dragon and points a finger heavenward while an adoring woman clutches a palm branch in her crossed hands. Both plates are so much too big even for this folio that their margins have had to be cropped to make them fit, and at first glance their effects seem unlike those of the ten plates indubitably by Barlow. Yet Vertue in his *Note Book*, the antiquarian bookseller Thomas Dodd in his sale catalogue (24 January 1809) and his *Connoisseurs Repository* [1825], and Croft-Murray and Hulton all attribute the portrait to Barlow without indicating any doubt (or offering any grounds for their certainty). And if Barlow did the portrait, he did the Theophila triumphant (to give it a short title). In spite of the differences between these two plates and the ten others, I have come to agree with the attribution to Barlow. Probably he designed and executed them to meet Benlowes' requirements for one of his earlier plans for the book. In a general way Theophila triumphant would serve as an illustration anywhere in the poem – it has no special relevance to Canto IX – but it seems more likely to have been conceived as a general illustrative frontispiece, a companion to the frontispiece portrait. Jenkins says that the two do occur as frontispieces in two extant copies of the book.

The difference in effect between these two plates and Barlow's series of illustrations for *Theophila* seems to arise from the two being engraved and etched, with the etched passages being bitten so lightly that the prints are hardly distinguishable from engravings. Nevertheless, the putti in the corners of the portrait and the accenting of hair, plants, and the dragon of the second plate are unmistakably

48) BARLOW, from Benlowes: *Theophila*, 281 × 181 mm.

Pro Liberis Libros.
Verè nostra quæ semper nostra

etched. On the other hand, the main series are fairly well-bitten tonal etchings. There is a good deal of burin work in them, too, as was common at the time. Once this difference is recognized, it is easy to match details in these two plates with similar ones in the series and in the rest of Barlow's work: the crinkly plants – almost a Barlow signature – the palm-leaves treated like the cattail leaves in the fables, the wings and faces of the putti of the portrait exactly repeated (to take the first example at hand) in the figure of Theophila in the illustration for Canto V and the angels in the Cantos I and VII plates, the profiles of Theophila in the plate for Canto V and in the Theophila triumphant, the latter's winged-head brooch and the cherubim in the Canto VII plate, the remarkable naturalism of the dragon, matched in England at this time only by Barlow's animals, including a dragon in Canto IV and a closely similar one in *Pelecanicidium*. Perhaps the best reason for believing that Barlow did these two plates is that there is no other conceivable candidate.

This amount of analysis to support the belief that Barlow is both artist and etcher-engraver of the Benlowes portrait and Theophila triumphant is justified by the excellence of both. As we have seen, Barlow is said to have been a pupil of William Shepherd, a portrait painter, and he did paint a portrait of General Monk and apparently one of Arthur, third Viscount Irwin. Against a background of the miserable engraved portraits by native artists such as Robert Vaughan, William Marshall, George Glover, and Thomas Cross, the Benlowes portrait dazzles by its lightness and grace. Gabriel Harvey said Benlowes had been 'a smudge [smart] piece of a handsome fellow'. The three-quarter head and shoulders of the poet has a double frame of laurel and boldly curling scroll-work. In the corners are two perhaps over-naturalistic putti; in the lower left corner is Benlowes' coat of arms, and in the lower right a balancing centaur shield, emblem of the poet maybe. An oval cartouche at the base of the design should have the poet's name engraved in it, but Benlowes did not get round to having the job done. The candid, sensitive face looking out of the clutter of ornamentation is one of the liveliest of portraits in the whole range of British etching, as it is one of the earliest.

It seems likely that Van Dyck's wonderful etched portraits are the direct inspiration for Barlow's portrait of Benlowes. They have much in common in their indifference to all but the face and in their free linear technique, with only moderate biting of deeper shadows. They have in common too a vibrancy missing even in the fine engraved translations of Van Dyck by Robert van Voerst. But Barlow's portrait is even more precisely akin to Van Dyck's own superb etching in the transcription of similar detail, as in the eyes, nose, and mouth of his portrait of Frans Snyders, and the loose treatment of hair, as in his self-portrait. (The underlying drawing of Benlowes' head is also virtually identical with that of Van

49) BARLOW, from *Theophila*, 272 × 175 mm.

50) BARLOW, from *Theophila*, 189 × 137 mm.

Dyck's oil painting of Charles I in the Louvre.) As noted in Chapter I, Barlow could have become acquainted with his etching technique through one of Van Dyck's former assistants or just from his prints.

The engraved quality (and, of course, the actual burin work) of the companion plate of Theophila triumphant gives it a chilly formal effect in comparison with Barlow's other ten illustrations. But it is not hard to see that with more biting and the resultant softening of lines and deepening of shadows it would probably take on much the same dramatic intensity as the best of the regular series. Theophila with head and hand raised in heavenly salute is a figure of dignity and repose; yet she keeps her foot firmly on the hideous, still writhing serpent of Evil. Above a delicately noted rose bush a woman, symbol of faith presumably, bends forward adoringly and in so doing adds rhythm to the composition. Had the portrait and this expression of the poem's main theme been printed as frontispieces on paper with adequate margins, with no other illustrations, *Theophila* would still have been a book of considerable distinction.

The Poet and the Illustrator

In spite of the vagaries in the writing of *Theophila* and assembling individual presentation and rebound copies, the role of Barlow as the chief illustrator and the only artist to address himself seriously to the task of illustrating the poem is unmistakable. Jenkins states that Benlowes had apparently written twelve cantos before he went off in 1648 to fight for King Charles. He seems to have commissioned Barlow to do his portrait and the Theophila triumphant frontispiece a good deal earlier when he was planning a much shorter poem. Sometime later, finding the two plates too modest in number if too large in size, he decided on a slightly less regal folio and commissioned Barlow to prepare ten illustrations – really frontispieces – for the cantos that then comprised what he thought would be the completed work. Or possibly the commission was for eight, and two more were added; the plates illustrating Cantos I, II, III, IV, VI and VIII have engraved on them the correct numbers. This plan seems not to have worked out smoothly, perhaps because Barlow was slow in delivering some of the plates or because Benlowes was too impatient to wait for them. Some copies of *Theophila* have only four of Barlow's plates, and some have his plates in relation to cantos which differ from those listed in the following discussion.

Although the etched illustrations are in the emblem-book tradition, they go beyond any of the usual 'devices'. They create dynamic situations in the allegory of Theophila's progression in grace, with occasional intrusions by the poet. All the evidence makes it seem a certainty that Benlowes conferred closely with Barlow about the illustrations. He may have made rough sketches, for Jenkins says that in addition to a lifelong addiction to fancy penmanship he 'certainly used to paint'. But if Benlowes had had the power to evoke complex scenes with figures and symbols in concrete pictorial terms, he would probably have done so in his poem. Nowhere does he employ any but micro-images. What in fact Barlow had to do, then, was not to illustrate generously described dramatic scenes in a work of imaginative literature such as *Paradise Lost* or *Pilgrim's Progress*. Together with what he could make out of the poem, he presumably had to develop a design that embodied what Benlowes *said* was the essential idea of each incoherent canto, an extraordinarily difficult achievement.

Each of the first six illustrations is related not to the text of the poem but in detail to four couplets engraved on a plate inserted below the illustration, on which, in emblem-book symbiosis, the couplets are also a commentary. Thus it seems that with either Barlow's drawings or proofs of the plates before him, Benlowes wrote six sets of verses and had them engraved before discovering that squeezing both plates on one page was unsightly. This may have induced him to discontinue the engraved verses after Canto VI. Otherwise he probably followed much the same process of collaboration with the artist in the preparation of the other four of the ten plates.

All of Barlow's plates except the one for Canto V are printed apart from the letterpress on the verso side of sheets slightly shorter than the printed pages. This separation was necessary in order to start each canto on the recto because the text of all the cantos except Canto IV happens to end on the verso. With Canto IV ending on the recto, the illustration for Canto V could go on the verso, with the text for Canto V beginning on the facing recto. Five of the miscellaneous prints previously listed are also printed separately, and four are on pages with text. (The Hollar 'Winter' is separate, but his 'Summer' is on a text page.)

The printing of the plates is a puzzle. Benlowes may have printed some, or even all except the two woodcuts, on his rolling-press. (Why else did he have it and Schoren?) But in view of the nature of etching and of the early state of the art in Britain, it would seem natural for Barlow to pull his own impressions, though only three years before he had written to Evelyn that etching was not his profession. Since, however, Norton was a printer of long experience, probably he handled the illustrations, both those in the text and those on separate sheets, as he would normally do. Benlowes might have taken the plates home afterwards – he doubtless had paid for them – and pulled a few impressions, but more probably he would have taken a stock of impressions along with printed sheets (it was usual for the printer to deliver unbound sheets to the booksellers) and contented

51) BARLOW, from *Theophila*, 191 × 135 mm.

52) BARLOW, drawing for *Theophila*, 191 × 135 mm.

himself with inserting them according to his whim as he made up what could not have been a large number of presentation copies for binding. It seems likely that both plates and flat sheets were destroyed when Brent Hall burned down in 1653.

Barlow's Ten Illustrations

The order of the Barlow plates in the following discussion is that in the British Library copy G.11598.

Barlow's first etching for Canto I, 'The Prelibation to the Sacrifice', is a be-guiling fusion of a captured moment and a baroque concept of eternity (fig. 50) (189 × 137 mm.). On the left the 'author musing' has the immediacy of a sketch from life. Indeed, the Bellini-like youth writing in a book with a foot on a globe looks a younger version of the Benlowes of the frontispiece. His coat of arms on two arches, as on the frontispiece portrait, identifies him as Benlowes. An eagle flies heavenward with his book, and Theophila in an ermine-trimmed gown holds a celestial sphere while an angel descends to crown her. All of this is spelled out emblem-book fashion in the appended engraved verse:

> *The Author musing here survay,*
> *How He may Theophil portray:*
> *Where Others Art surpast you find,*
> *They draw the Body, He the Mind.*
> *The World's beneath his Foot; while Shee*
> *Heav'n by the Heav'nly Sphere, does see.*
> *A Crown is reacht Her from the Skies,*
> *Up with his Book an Eagle flies.*

In the etching for Canto II, 'The Humiliation', Theophila kneels in prayer before a fountain, a symbol of 'Christ the Fount', encircled by an ape, a delightful dragon, a wolf, a snake, a leopard, a bear, and a boar, all snarling viciously – i.e., she is 'besieg'd with deadly Sinnes'—(fig. 51) (191 × 135 mm.). Lightly sketched in the background are Adam and Eve, first with the serpent and then driven out of the Garden. A comparison of this illustration with the original drawing (fig. 52) reveals that at least fourteen years before he published his Aesop Barlow was a master in both drawing and etching animals.

With something of the improbability with which Bach fashioned so much of his noble *St. Matthew Passion* out of tearful hymns, Barlow takes whatever specifica-tions Benlowes provided to create the tender pietistic design for Canto III, 'The Restauration' (fig. 53) (185 × 134 mm.). At the left King David plays his harp, while (back centre) Theophila, holding Moses's tablets, raises her eyes to angels

53) BARLOW, from *Theophila*, 185 × 134 mm.

54) BARLOW, from *Theophila*, 186 × 133 mm.

showering flowers of grace upon her. On the right stands a naked bleeding Christ-like man at whose feet are a bagpipe, a horn, a cithern, and a terrestrial sphere crowned by a fool's cap. From a female statue (above) with crossed arms tears descend on the man below – 'Teares from sad Penitence doe flow/On Man, who bleeds for joys below'. Barlow's management of this awkward scene is a triumph. David is kept in half-light. Theophila with the tablets at the top of steps is in a full light, but she is unobtrusively small. A statue of Penitence is wholly dark. Thus the figure of Man is brightly lighted except for his shadowed compassion-ate face. The likeness to Christ is no accident; through penitence Man becomes Christ-like.

The fourth of the series is a turbulent design of Theophila as the soul fighting temptations, Canto IV, 'The Inamoration' (fig. 54) (186 × 133 mm.). An angel supports her on one side; on the other she is assailed by a satanic rout. A phoenix amid flames, a winged flaming heart, a pair of doves, an anchor, and other symbols of faith and hope on one side and skulls, a crown, and other symbols of evil on the other make this illustration and its accompanying verse the most emblematic of the series. High in the sky Theophila is borne by angels toward the crucified Christ. This illustration has been ruined in most copies by over-inking. Why did Benlowes tolerate such unsatisfactory work unless the sheet, the only one with the plate on the verso, had already been printed? That Theophila and one of the devils are shown left-handed is merely a slip on Barlow's part, not evidence of borrowing, as has been suggested. Unless anticipatory reversing takes place in the drawing where necessary, as it has in the plates for Cantos I and III, figures will be left-handed, and time sequences will seem to move backwards, as the two Adam and Eve incidents seem to in the plate for Canto II. The last thing imaginable here is borrowing. Apart from the abominable printing of some impressions of this plate, it is a brilliantly successful projection of both the visual detail and the emotional conflict, so circumstantially set forth in the engraved text (on which the engraved number also prints backwards):

The Soule against Temptations fights,
Whom Death and Hell present with frights:
The World with Wealth and Honour courts;
The Fleshes Glasse invites to Sports:
But Theophil by Faith her Shield,
And Hopes firm Anchor stands the Field;
Accompany'd with Grace and Love,
By Angels She does upward move.

55) BARLOW, from *Theophila*, 194 × 137 mm.

56) BARLOW, from *Theophila*, 194 × 135 mm.

In addition to the commentary for Canto I, further evidence that Benlowes wrote his six engraved commentaries with the designs before him is the explicit language of the one for Canto V, 'The Representation':

View here the Authors high Designe,
His Book displai'd, his Tapers shine,
Th' Athenian Bird, the Dog, and Cat,
Which Watchfull Study intimate.
Theophl'a doth before Him stand
Amused [gazing intently] *with erected Hand;*
And, like an Eagle, upward flies,
Rapt by bright Angels to the Skies.

It is a concept even more quaintly personal than the one for Canto I. Again identified by his coat of arms, the youthful poet, sitting up in an alcove bed with his book opened in one hand, beholds a vision of a winged Theophila in a radiance (191 × 137 mm.). A candle on a tall stand, an owl, a cat, and a dog add a curious realism to the scene, while a screaming eagle sets up a tension at variance with the poet's faraway look. The celestial city in the heaven may be derived from an emblem book. Partly by reason of its uncluttered clarity, this is one of the most attractive of the *Theophila* designs. Never before had so lifelike an image of a dog and a cat (Barlow's own, one cannot help thinking) been seen in an English book. Yet the main accomplishment lies in the conviction that what the text so flatly states is, within the conventions of art, actually taking place: out of the poet's contemplative imagination Theophila stands forth, woman, goddess, and angel, and then in a sort of cinematic sequence points upward to herself 'rapt by bright Angels to the Skies'.

Further evidence that Barlow's illustrations were at least drawn before Benlowes wrote the engraved commentary comes at the end of the verse for Canto VI, 'The Association', in the reference to the slight detail of a triangle that extends beyond the top of the design (187 × 138 mm.):

Here Abraham, David, Daniel stand,
Luke, Judah, Moses, in whose Hand
The Law is held; The Virgins see,
Martyrs, Apostles, Hierarchy:
An Angell tends with Message down:
By Triangle, part drawn, is shown
The Trinitie, whose Mysteries
No Mortalls Knowledge can comprise.

Benlowes' lines give no hint of Barlow's clever organization, both logical and visual, of nearly four dozen figures. (Benlowes names only six of Barlow's seven prophets.) The individual figures are necessarily sketchy, but are established with economy, variety, and animation in a chalice-like pattern that must have delighted the symbol-avid Benlowes.

We come now to the four Barlow illustrations which are unaccompanied by engraved explication. As we have said, Benlowes must have discussed these four designs with Barlow as carefully as the others, even after giving up the engraved explanatory plates. They reveal the same sensitive grasp of Benlowes' iconographic intent as the preceding six.

The unnumbered design (188 × 137 mm.) for Canto VII, 'The Contemplation', seems applicable to the text of the poem:

> *She launcheth into shoarless Seas of Light,*
> *Inexplicable, Infinite!*
> *Whose Beams both strike her blinde, and renovate*
> *her Sight!*

Jenkins says that it is found in this position in all good copies of the book. Theophila, having ascended above the clouds, lifts her eyes rapturously to a radiant symbol of the Trinity, while an Angel in flight offers her a large O, symbol of 'immense Eternitie', which 'an indeterminable Circle art'.

Barlow followed this plate with a companion design for Canto VIII, 'The Admiration' (188 × 136 mm.). On the left, lifted by two angels, Theophila aspires toward heaven, in which hang two triangles and a star of David enclosing a circle. On the right condemned souls, escorted by devils, tumble into the fiery mouth of Hell. Perhaps because the wings of the angels seem so capable of sustaining them in flight and because of the uncompromising nakedness of the damned, this two-way illustration achieves an unexpected sense of conviction. Benlowes must have worked out its contents with Barlow, for the text offers no equivalent.

The plate for Canto IX in BL:G.11598 is the large Theophila triumphant already discussed. The title of the canto is 'The Recapitulation', but it is a further rhapsody of 100 Latin couplets and 100 parallel English couplets followed by more Latin verse. One imagines that it was not a part of Benlowes' plan until after Barlow had illustrated the first eight cantos.

Although the paging and canto numbering are continuous, at Canto X Benlowes recognizes that he has completed *Theophila* by discontinuing that title. Barlow's last two illustrations reflect this change. They are uniform in size, a little larger than the preceding ones (thus matching the facing type-page better), and similar in style, but they are treated as illustrations for separate poems with different moods and central characters. Strong evidence that they were executed later than the others is the use for the first time in Barlow's work of close horizontal-line shading, especially in clothing, a technique used also in his next book, Denny's *Pelecanicidium.*

The main title for Cantos X and XI becomes 'The Vanitie of the World'. The Canto X special heading is 'The Abnegation'. Benlowes announces in the first page of the text:

> *But, here my sharpned Muse shall entertain*
> *The Scourges of Satyrick Vein,*
> *To lash the World, in which such store of Vices reign.*
> *No Grandee Patron court I, nor entice*
> *Love-glances from enchanting Eyes,*
> *Nor Blandishments from Lisping Wantons vocall Spice ...*

Benesch selects Barlow's illustration (fig. 55) (194 × 137 mm.) for special praise:

> One of the most powerful inventions in Barlow's series is the allegorical scene which shows the religious man resisting the temptations of worldly power and wealth, of love and vanity, in order to strive for the crown of eternal bliss. In the foreground the Duke [emperor?] with a halo of daggers piercing his hat presents a fantastic sight. The half-length figures rise in a majestic crescendo; various geometrical patterns, such as circles, spheres, and ellipses, play their part in the composition. The figures strive concentrically toward a celestial vision which emits a fan of rays. This is a work filled with the gloomy monumentality and mystical spirit of Puritanism.

One doubts that Barlow would have thought of precisely this allegory without some help from the poet, but one cannot imagine Benlowes inventing the design at all. The somewhat similar second illustration for *Pelecanicidium* shows that Barlow could think in these terms by himself. Certainly the details do not emerge from a reading of 'The Abnegation'. Barlow may have used Benlowes, approaching fifty, as his model for the religious man in this design. How he gives a rhythmic spin to the composition while building up 'monumentality' is worth noting. A counter-clockwise half-circle starting at the man's raised hand runs down through Vanity, a young woman holding a mirror and fool's cap, through Greed, hunched under a bag of money, to Power (the 'Grandee Patron') with his crown secured in a double sense by swords and a musket. A clockwise semicircle flows down the religious man's left arm, the wanton lady Love clutching it, over the elliptical stone on a plinth, along the emperor's left arm to his hand at six o'clock in relation to the religious man's at twelve. The sword hilts and points and the musket sticking out all round the emperor's crown form the spokes at the hub of this wheel. The interlocking construction of two forward thrusting figures with three erect ones and the play of light and dark add a great deal to making this one of the most sophisticated designs invented by an English book illustrator for three centuries. The original drawing is bound in the Victoria and Albert Museum copy of *Theophila*.

The main theme for Canto XI continues to be the vanity of the world. In the British Library copy of *Theophila* that we are using the illustration for Canto XI, 'The Disincantation', is the one for Canto I repeated, further evidence of the confusion attending publication of these last cantos.

The new main title at Canto XII becomes 'The Sweetnesse of Retirement, or The Happinesse of a Private Life', and the superfluous heading is 'The Segregation'. This is the only instance where the text begins on the verso. Although the impression of the etching (fig. 56) (194 × 135 mm.) in BL:G.11598 is woefully weak and some of the lines have been reinforced by a burin, the illustration is a wonderfully articulated pastoral, a perfect, if belated, graphic realization of what British poets had been lyrical about since Spenser's *Shepherds Calendar*. In the foreground an old shepherd attended by his dog and flock is addressed by a handsome courtly youth, the poet in a new role. He is dandified by the addition of ruffles at the bottom of the same sober knee-length suit worn by the pious hero of Canto X. Beyond, in a sequence arbitrarily not receding into the background, are scenes of the youth picnicking beside a spring-fed stream, a country woman milking her cows, a boy driving in another cow, a chapel, a man tending hop vines, two figures nutting, peasants and their thatched cottage, and a hunt. Nothing so idyllic, with detail like the charming sheep and suckling lamb, had ever before appeared in an English book. The illustration seems likely to have been designed by Barlow with little aid from Benlowes and to be based on his reading of the first two eclogue-like pages of Canto XIII, which continues the theme of Canto XII under the slightly different main title 'The Pleasure of Retirement'. The Virgilian scene does not reflect the religious fervour of Canto XII or the rest of Canto XIII at all.

Because they are bound in certain copies of *Theophila* from which Barlow's have been removed, we should mention two of Jan Baptist Gaspars' plates. (See Chapter II.) They were etched one year later for *The Extravagant Shepherd* (1653), a translation by John Davies of Kidwelly, another friend of Benlowes. They are delightful, but they do not belong to *Theophila*.

Benesch says about the etchings by Barlow for *Theophila*, 'The illustrations show a grandeur of imagination, produced with all the freshness of a young artist.' Here for the first time within the covers of a printed book an English-born etcher-illustrator follows and surpasses Marcus Gheeraerts the elder: the designs are complex and naturalistic, mastery of anatomy and emotional expressiveness are matters of fact, and wild and domestic creatures spring to life. But most extraordinary is the subordination of the innovative naturalism of drawing and tonal effects to the function of illustration, to serve faithfully the purposes of the poet, and odd as Benlowes' purposes may be, Barlow succeeds without ever sinking into the disaster of bathos. Yet Barlow was probably only twenty-five years old when he designed and etched these ten plates.

Theophila would have been a brilliant example of a successful illustrated book if Benlowes had kept all but Barlow's illustrations out. They have to be 'read' in the light of the emblem imagery in which the poem is steeped, but they also reflect Barlow's own unaffectedness, as in his introduction of animals into the religious milieu. No matter what the limitations of the poet (and occasionally the printing of the plates), Barlow traces the mystical progress of the soul in designs unsurpassed in English book illustration for exquisite drawing and sensitive etching. He penetrates to the sincerity at the heart of Benlowes' mystical fervour, eccentricity, and banality, and gives it graphic utterance in etchings worthy to stand beside any ever made by an Englishman and designs that by themselves make him the first British master of interpretive book illustration and one of the best of any period.

CHAPTER VII

The Interpretive Illustrations
of Wenceslaus Hollar

A LTHOUGH HE SPENT less than half his working life in London, the great
Czech etcher Wenceslaus (Vaclav, Wenzel) Hollar (1607–1677) is an important figure in English book illustration. His reputation rests on his wonderful topographical and architectural etchings, but to make a living he squandered much of his unique talent copying the paintings and drawings of other artists, including Barlow. Recently his fine watercolours have come to be better known and prized. A great many of his more than 2,700 plates were issued within the covers of books, but they are almost all really independent prints – the text might be said to illustrate them. Only a small fraction of Hollar's immense output can be called interpretive illustration, and it has received little critical attention.

The facts of Hollar's life are well known and can be quickly summarized. He was born in Prague, where Gilles (Aegidius) Sadeler may have directed him toward etching. He studied and worked in Germany and joined the entourage of the Earl of Arundel to record his travels on the Continent. The Earl brought him to England in 1637 to make drawings and etchings of paintings and other art objects in the great collection at Arundel House, but he soon extended his activities, etched a number of portraits, and secured access to the Court. In the Civil War he took up arms for Charles I and then worked in exile in Antwerp from 1644 to 1652. Somehow he was allowed to return to London and even worked for Cromwell's printer, John Field. In spite of his incredible diligence and productivity and the great popularity of his minutely detailed etchings, he remained poor and exploited. (Place says in his letter to Vertue 20 May 1716 that Hollar's left eye was defective, an extreme handicap for an etcher.) As a result of his brilliant etchings of London scenes, he was appointed 'King's Scenographer' and in 1669 was sent to make drawings of Tangiers, which Charles II had got as part of Catherine of Braganza's dowry. He died indigent and was buried at St. Margaret's, Westminster, with a note in the church record that he was famous.

The books of Urzidil, Hind, Van Eerde, and others have dealt thoroughly with Hollar's career. We need only touch on some aspects to serve as background for his interpretive illustrations. An orderly soul, Hollar signed and sometimes dated and even 'placed' a large number of plates and when appropriate included the designer's name with scrupulous care. This conscientiousness is extremely helpful. Unfortunately, he frequently forgot, and we cannot safely infer that the absence of another artist's name means that Hollar was both designer and etcher. Moreover, he uses *fecit* sometimes to mean *sculpsit* and sometimes *invenit et sculpsit*. The close imitation of his etching style by his pupils and others like Francis Place is also a source of possible error in discussing what seems unsigned work by Hollar.

57) HOLLAR, from *Ornatus muliebris Anglicanus*, 127 × 69 mm.

Hollar As Factual Draughtsman

Hollar was primarily a literal recorder, nearer in spirit to a modern professional photographer than to a print-maker, though photographers today are more self-consciously 'artistic' than he ever was. The charm of his etchings lies in the fastidious manner with which he records what he saw (or imagined he would see). The effects that dazzle us seldom have any of the emotional colouring of the prints by his greater contemporary Rembrandt.

This combination of the photographic eye and the exquisite touch is apparent in two fashion series printed in book form without text soon after Hollar's arrival in England: *Ornatus muliebris Anglicanus, or The Seuerall Habits of English Women, from the Nobilitie to the contry Woman, as they are in these times, 1640,* followed by the companion volume *Theatru Mulierum* (1643) for all of Europe, which slyly includes three monks. The engraved title-page for the latter advertises 'This sett of 48 prints 4 s . . . delineatae et aqua forti aeri sculptae' by Hollar. These must be among the earliest references in England to etching by means of acid and to the term print for the impression of a plate. The lovingly rendered fashion plates are valuable documents in the history of social classes as well as of costumes (fig. 57). It is characteristic of the conscientious Czech that each face gives the impression of being drawn from life.

Through the years Hollar etched some of his own manuals not only to help students and artisans but also to satisfy the rising interest in the natural world. In Antwerp he etched *Muscarum Scarabeorum* (1646), a book of butterflies at all stages, after drawings he had made in London from examples in the Arundel collection. Another manual is his *Animalium, Ferarum, & Bestiarum, Florum, Fructuum, Muscarum, Vermiumq* (1663). And John Overton advertised that his later edition, *Four Hundred New Sorts of Birds, Beasts, Flowers, Fruits, Fish, Flyes, Worms, Landskips, Ovals, & Histories,* 'lively coloured', was easily adapted for use by 'all sorts of Gentlewomen and Schoolmistresses'. This is one of the earliest examples of a book with hand-coloured illustrations published in England. Jacques le Moyne's *La clef des champs pour trouver plusieurs Animaux, tant Bestes qu' Oyseaux, avec plusieurs Fleurs & Fruitz* (Imprime aux Blackfriers, 1586) with ninety-four coloured woodcuts is earlier.

Much more dramatic and important as original records appearing in books are plates showing historical occasions such as the trials of the Earl of Strafford and Archbishop Laud and the Coronation of Charles II in Westminster Abbey. These plates are graphic journalism of the highest order. Equally valuable as social records, though not so filled with drama, are the many extraordinary etchings of buildings and places Hollar contributed to books by the new breed of anti-

PROSPECT OF THE CANCELL
from the East.

58) HOLLAR, from Ashmole: *Institutions, Laws and Ceremonies*
of the most Noble Order of the Garter, 169 × 266 mm.

quarians Dodsworth, Dugdale, Ashmole, and Sandford.

Some of Hollar's finest architectural plates are in Elias Ashmole's folio *Institution, Laws & Ceremonies of the most Noble Order of the Garter* (1672) (fig. 58). Some of the double-spread plates are among the splendours of etching, particularly the several prospects of Windsor Castle, the interior of St. George's Chapel, and a royal dinner scene in St. George's Hall. Hollar dates a number of the plates: the earliest 1663, the latest 1672. He also indicates that he invented as well as etched almost all and signs two with the grand empty Carolean title 'Scenographus Regius'. He punctiliously assigns the original authorship of a close-up view of Windsor Castle from the river to Christopher Wren and a rearrangement of a procession of Queen Elizabeth and the Knights Companions of the Order of the Garter to 'Marcus Gerard'. Perhaps he had access to Gheeraerts' multi-plate etching of 1576 at Windsor when on 25 May 1659, according to Ashmole's diary, 'I went to Windsor, and took Mr. Hollar with me to take views of the Castle'.

In their way three of the half-dozen plates that Hollar etched for a great Bible printed by John Field at Cambridge for Ogilby (1660) are even more impressive, since they are necessarily imaginary. They are Solomon's Temple (370 × 510 mm.) with sacrificial rites taking place in the courtyard (fig. 59), the Temple of Jerusalem (385 × 510 mm.) in the centre of the city, and then one of the most astonishing of all English etchings, a panoramic view of Jerusalem seen slightly from above with Mount Sion in the middle, made up of the impressions of two plates glued together to pull out to equal two double-spreads (390 × 1220 mm.). In these three plates the infinite elaboration of cunning detail that Hollar had never seen is a stunning *tour-de-force*. To these plates must be added the double-spread re-creation of Persepolis in Sir Thomas Herbert's *Some Years' Travels into Africa and Asia* (1665).

A dozen years before publication Hollar began work on Francis Sandford's *A Genealogical History of the Kings of England 1066–1677* (1677), which he completed with some help from Barlow and Gaywood. It is one of his masterpieces of incredible on-the-spot draughtsmanship, especially his double-spreads of the tombs of the Duke of Albemarle in Westminster Abbey and Gilbert, Archbishop of Canterbury, in the Cathedral. He signed the latter for posterity 'W. Hollar fecit, aqua forti, A° 1665, Aetat: 58: compl:'. Before leaving this cursory review of Hollar's work as a factual draughtsman, it is fair to mention that he was an excellent cartographer, that he added many grace notes to Ogilby's geographical works, and that his historic long etching of London before the Fire appeared first in Richard Blome's *Britannia* (1673). His numerous title-pages are often enlivened by etched figures that set them apart from the frozen efforts of Marshall and other engravers.

59) HOLLAR, from *The Bible* (John Field 1660), (detail).

139

Illustrations Etched after Designs by Others

Hollar probably felt no sense of inferiority in the secondary role of etcher of other men's illustrations. Artists in the sixteenth and seventeenth centuries were trained in a rigorous system to do all sorts of jobs. But it was also a period when the reproductive engraver and etcher enjoyed a status sometimes higher than that of the designer, and sometimes better paid.

In order to perpetuate the marvellous Holbein *Dance of Death* (Lyon, 1538) woodcuts, Hollar etched reproductions (74 × 53 mm.) of thirty of them. He transferred the last, a death's head on a shield, to go with the new engraved title, *Mortalium nobilitas*. Because these small plates are craftily enlarged by hardly noticeable enclosure within a few borders drawn by Abraham van Diepenbeeck, several of which are dated 1651, it seems likely that the collection was published in 1651 or 1652 but that the reproductions were made while Hollar was still in Antwerp. The British Library copy of *Mortalium nobilitas* (G.2298) has in the front a portrait of Holbein etched by Hollar after the self-portrait in the Arundel collection. It is dated 1647, *i.e.*, while Hollar was in Antwerp. It is said to be 'inserted' in this edition, but there could hardly be a better reason for Hollar to etch a portrait of Holbein of just this size. Of the same size and equally fresh is an etched copy of Joannes Myssens' Antwerp portrait of Hollar clearly by Hollar himself. Hollar's faithfulness to Holbein's designs is his tribute to his great predecessor. Minor variations in the reversed etchings suggest that he did not use tracings, but probably he did. The etchings, of course, achieve precision of detail and depth and softness of shadows not in the nature of woodcuts. The same plates and borders were used in a Paris edition [1680?] with H i (*Holbein invenit*) along with Hollar's initials on the inner plates. These original plates without the borders reappear over a century later in a worn condition in an edition said to be edited by Douce [1794?]. An oval copy of the Hollar portrait has engraved beneath it the incorrect 'etched by Barlow'.

In Chapter IV we saw that one of Hollar's early assignments on returning to Cromwell's London from Antwerp was the etching of forty-two of a hundred and one large illustrations and numerous decorative designs for Ogilby's first illustrated folio, the second edition of his translation of Virgil's works (1654). At least seventy-four, perhaps one hundred, of the designs are by Francis Cleyn. Hollar's etching bestows an intimacy on the large multiple-event illustrations that is not present in the competent but impersonal engravings by Pierre Lombart, who did most of the rest of the plates. Both etcher and engraver fall short of the heroic in their treatment of Virgil's characters. (Hollar's features have much the same insignificance as those of Gheeraerts' faces.) Hollar's short etched lines achieve softer effects, more agreeable gradations of darkness and light, that pull the designs together in a way that Lombart's longer, harsher lines do not. Lombart presents the event, Hollar realizes the scene. He takes unusual pains with trees and foliage, and, of course, his architecture, as in fig. 59, always becomes a dynamic element in its own right.

We cannot help feeling frustrated, however, that Hollar's part in this imposing Virgil is not the major one. Nor is he even the sole interpreter of the drawings. Yet the experience must have been an important one for him. It was his first ambitious exercise in the illustration of imaginative literature, albeit at second-hand, and it must have made him think seriously about the special nature of interpretive illustration.

After the Virgil, the monument of Hollar's skill in turning other men's draw-ings into etched illustrations is Sir Robert Stapylton's translation, with a parallel Latin text, of *Mores Hominum. The Manners of Men Described in sixteen Satyrs by Juvenal* (R. Hodgkinsonne, 1660). Hollar etched the frontispiece and the sixteen illustrations (*c.* 280 × 200 mm.), of which he may have designed two. On the title-page Stapylton says that he has used the 'most Authentick Copy, lately printed by command of the King of France. Whereunto is added the Invention of seventeen Designes in Picture. With Arguments to the Satyrs. As also Explana-tions to the Designes in English and Latine'. In addition to doing a portrait of Stapylton, engraved by Pierre Lombart, Johan Danckerts, a new-come Dutch painter, designed the illustrations for Satires I–VII, and Robert Streater, an early English landscape painter, drew the half-title frontispiece and the illustra-tions for Satires IX, X, XII, XIII, XV. The drawings for Satires VIII and XI by Barlow we have already discussed. It seems odd to bring him in for only two illustrations. Therefore Hollar's *fecit* on the plates for Satires XIV and XVI may mean that he also designed them. Hollar's strongly personalized style brings about a harmony that the drawings could not have had. Yet the illustrations, archaically visualizing the chief points of each satire, as in Barlow's plate XI (fig. 42), have so strong a family resemblance that a guiding mind, or source, seems prob-able. Michael van der Gucht copied the series on much smaller engraved plates for the Tonson edition translated by Dryden and 'Other Eminent Hands' (1697).

A pleasant example of Hollar's secondary work is *The Office of the Holy Week According to the Missal and Roman Breviary* (1670), translated from the French by W.K.B. [Sir W. K. Blount] and printed in Paris by the 'Widow Chrestien'. It contains seven signed etchings (132 × 81 mm.) of the Passion. Four are after designs by Stella and Palma (*i.e.*, from paintings in a London collection?). Because of the plenitude of Passion designs, the rest may not be Hollar's inventions, although he signs them all, another instance where he creates doubt by his ambiguous use of *fecit*. It would be difficult, however, to find another Passion series by an English illustrator that has the harmony, warmth, and dignity of this one. Only the derivative nature of the four designs and the possibility that the others are copied, too, restrains praise of Hollar's work here.

As we have seen in Chapter V, in addition to etching some of Barlow's bird and animal instructional prints, Hollar etched entirely only two of the plates in Barlow's *Severall Wayes of Hunting, Hawking, & Fishing* (1671). In 1676, the year before his death, and as early as 1672 Hollar etched many plates after the designs of R. Hall for Robert Thoroton's *Antiquities of Nottinghamshire* (1677). Most are of churches and stately homes, including two-page spreads. One might wish that the old etcher could have been doing plates that offered more freedom; yet he never skimps a stone or cornice in these unexciting architectural subjects.

Minor Original Illustrations

For Isaac Ambrose's *Prima & Ultima: The First & Last Things* (1640), printed by Samuel Brown in London before he went into exile at The Hague, Hollar provided a title-page and six etched illustrations (*c.* 102 × 92 mm.). The 399 pages of lugubrious sermons have a plate as frontispiece to 'First Things' and to each of the six parts of 'Last Things'. They are worth noting only because they show that Hollar could interpret text: he conducts a sort of pilgrim's progress from 'Life's Lease' to 'Heavens Happinesse'.

The eight illustrations for *All the memorable & wonderstrikinge Parlamentary* [sic] *Mercies effected . . . unto this our English Nation . . A° 1641 & 1642* [Sept. 1642] are Hollar's main venture into journalism. The plates (123 × 93 mm.) are divided in the middle so that they record sixteen scenes, each with an engraved caption, the only text. For all his loyalty to the King, Hollar dispassionately records pro-Parliament incidents such as 'The rising of Prentises and Sea-men on Southwark side to assault the Arch-bishops of Canterburys House at Lambeth' and the beheading of Strafford on Tower Hill. But after depicting the demolition of the cross in Cheapside on 2 May 1643 and the burning of the book of sports on Sunday 10 May, he may have left to join the Royalist forces. These cuts with additions appeared in later similar works. The chronicler, perhaps John Vicars, of *A sight of yᵉ Trans-actions of these latter yeares Emblemized with engrauen plats which men may read with out spectacles* [1646] says it is 'illustrated with neat and pertinent pictures and figures', an early use of the word illustrate in the modern sense. In 1648 in *True Information of the Beginning and Cause of all our Troubles* some of these plates appear cut in half but also with Hollar's two-compartment plate of the battle of Edgehill and of a fleet at sea, which must have accidentally been left out of *Parliamentary Mercies*.

A Solemn League and Covenant (1643) is an oddity. It consists of ten sheets printed sideways on one side only. Eight of the sheets have small etched designs (102 × 147 mm.) filling in the space around engraved text. The unsigned work is Covenanter propaganda, but it seems Hollar's. A unique example at Windsor Castle shows that all of the designs have been etched on one plate and the printing effected by masking out all but the design for the desired page.

The Second Edition of Ogilby's Aesop Paraphras'd (*1665*)

As we have seen, Strafford's downfall drove John Ogilby back to England from Dublin and into his third career, that of an author. The success of his octavo translation of Virgil (1649) and his original paraphrases of Aesop (1651), illustrated by Francis Cleyn, encouraged him to enter his fourth career as publisher on a grand scale – the *Works of Virgil* (1654), the *Iliad* (1660), the Bible (1660), the *Entertainment* (1661, 1662), and the *Odyssey* (1665). He had engaged Hollar to assist in some of these ventures. Now, fourteen years after the Cleyn Aesop and eleven after the Virgil, Ogilby published his second edition of *The Fables of Aesop Paraphras'd in Verse: Adorn'd with Sculpture, and Illustrated with Annotations* (1665).

The second edition of *Aesop Paraphras'd* is another luxurious folio, printed by Thomas Roycroft, the leading London printer of the day, in large type with wide margins for occasional elucidations, and necessarily it had to have a larger set of plates appropriate to the page size. Recalling his luck as a boy, Ogilby set about financing the high costs by a lottery. (Ewen and Schuchard give the details of this and the 1668 lottery.) Ogilby received help from the King, at no cost to His Majesty's purse. Anticipating the Copyright Act of 1709, a royal decree dated 25 May 1665, printed with the front matter, prohibits anyone to reprint any of the 'fair volumes' published by Ogilby, now by royal patent 'Master of Our Revels in Irelande', or 'to Copy or Counterfeit any [of] the Sculptures or Ingravements therein, within the Term of Fifteen years' without Ogilby's consent. This may be the earliest recognition in England of any wrong in 'counterfeiting' graphic designs.

To be sure that the illustrations met the high standards of this opulent edition, Ogilby relied on his old associate Hollar, now universally esteemed though still ill-rewarded. Hollar had never been called on to invent illustrations for a work of imaginative literature, with the possible exception of the two unassigned plates in the Juvenal. This handicap could not have bothered either Ogilby or Hollar: it was apparently understood that Hollar's assignment was not to invent new motifs but to transmute Cleyn's leaden images into golden ones – and in the main he did. One might imagine that Hollar welcomed the task with special pleasure. He was already an admirer of Marcus Gheeraerts' *De warachtighe Fabulen der Dieren* designs, for in the British Museum are his facsimile etchings of four of them. One he inscribes as from Aegidius Sadeler's exact copies of Gheeraerts' plates in his *Theatrum Morum* (Prague, 1608 [1609]), which Hollar might well have known as a youth and must have known if in fact he studied with Sadeler. The others are from the originals (Bruges, 1567) with Dutch inscriptions. Whether or not Hollar did only these four plates and whether or not they were part of a projected edition, he had paid studious attention to Gheeraerts' illustrations. Furthermore, as we shall soon see, he now had by him one of the several editions of Aesopic fables containing Gheeraerts' original plates, which he used as models when Cleyn's seemed inadequate.

The Division of Labour between Hollar and Dirk ('Roderigo') Stoop

---

Ogilby ruined what would have been one of the most magnificent illustrated volumes ever published in England by hiring Dirk ('Roderigo') Stoop (1610?–1686?) to share the task with Hollar. A native of Utrecht, Stoop came to England from Portugal as court painter to Catherine of Braganza in 1662 when she married Charles II. To identify himself with his royal patroness, no doubt, he called himself 'Roderigo' and used the abbreviation 'R°' in his signature on six of the *Aesop Paraphras'd* plates. A painter and etcher of considerable experience, like Cleyn he proved an uninspired illustrator and an unattractive etcher. We cannot blame Ogilby unduly. The use of more than one artist and more than one engraver was a not unusual way to get an elaborate edition out on time, as we saw in the instance of Stapylton's Juvenal. Ogilby may have been impressed by the stranger's reputation, and he may also have thought that hiring him would help his cause at Court, as possibly it did. Or, knowing that his neighbour Barlow was also at work on an Aesop, he may have taken on the Dutch artist to help out the burdened Hollar and speed up publication. Anyway, that is the way it was. Ogilby beat Barlow to publication, a matter of some consequence with two so similar expensive books.

A just appreciation of the work of Hollar and Stoop must begin with the following analysis of their sources. Ogilby's 1665 *Aesop Paraphras'd* contains eighty-one numbered plates (*c.* 220–50 × 165–95 mm.) for eighty-two fables. (The last one is new.) In a 30 mm. blank space at the bottom of each plate Ogilby apparently intended to engrave dedications to subscribers, as he had in the Virgil, but he was not able to carry the plan through. Hollar mechanically followed Cleyn in putting the two designs for Fables XIV and XV on one plate. For some reason Lombart engraved a slightly larger version of the Lely portrait of Ogilby in place of the one by Faithorne in the Virgil, and Hollar etched a free enlargement of Cleyn's Aesop frontispiece to face the dedication to Thomas, Earl of Ossory, 'Lord Deputy of His Majesties Kingdom of Ireland'.

Of the plates, Hollar etched fifty-seven (illustrating fifty-eight fables), and Stoop etched twenty-four. Hollar bases forty-four of his designs on Cleyn's (mainly based on Gheeraerts' series), nine directly on Gheeraerts, and four on both, and for Ogilby's new fable he drew an original illustration. Stoop follows Cleyn without meaningful deviation. Together their sources are Cleyn sixty-seven, Gheeraerts nine, combined four, and original one.

Stoop merely enlarges twenty-four of Cleyn's plates without showing the slightest inclination to improve them, except that in 'The Birds and Beasts' he introduces Gheeraerts' dog, which Cleyn had overlooked or perhaps deliberately left out. He does not try to reproduce them exactly, but the changes he makes have no significance. Sometimes he reverses the designs, and sometimes he does not. His unoriginal and unprepossessing copies of Cleyn represented the scenes, perhaps to the satisfaction of the readers, and may charitably be examined no further. He illustrated no other English books.

Hollar's Illustrations for Aesop Paraphras'd

Hollar's use of sources for his illustrations is complex. Some of the motifs that he takes from Cleyn he finds essentially satisfactory, and he merely redraws them, not always with as much improvement as one would expect. Some of his animals, the fox in the fable of 'The Fox and the Crow' for example, are not a great deal more convincing than Cleyn's. The half dozen or so designs with a considerable amount of foliage in the foreground tend to be his least distinguished, largely because the effects he gets by rendering leaves by means of curlicues are unrealistic and monotonous. So sometimes are the large areas of cross-hatching of unparticularized foreground. And occasionally dark animal and human figures lose interest by being placed unwisely against dark cross-hatched shadows.

More often, happily, Hollar takes over Cleyn's designs, adds nothing essential, yet makes them infinitely more appealing. For 'The Eagle and the Daw' Ogilby introduces a marble tomb in place of the rock the eagle drops the oyster on. Hollar reproduces Cleyn's inexplicably isolated tomb exactly but turns his sketchy background into a spacious harbour with ships, defended by a towered fortress.

Hollar's almost literal reproduction (fig. 60) of Cleyn's 'Fox and Ape' design (fig. 61) is one of the most striking illustrations in the book. Ogilby has the French ape try to beguile the fox of Spain into cutting his cloak short so that he

can lengthen his own apparel with the remnant. Then they will both be in fashion. (This refers to Louis XIV's intrigues about Spain's European possessions, but Ogilby's mild moral is that we all prize our own manners.) Except for a few details – the spectacles on the fox, the muff slung over the shoulder of the ape, and the exchange of the hats – Hollar does nothing but draw the two costumed animals much more elegantly and ever so much more entertainingly.

61) CLEYN, from *Aesop Paraphras'd* (1651), 145 × 90 mm.

60) HOLLAR, from Ogilby: *Aesop Paraphras'd* (1665), 221 × 164 mm.

In the main, however, Hollar adapts Cleyn's designs with sensitive changes. In his illustration for 'The Court Mouse and the Countrie Mouse' (fig. 62) Hollar builds up the opulence of the city larder by turning a useless stool in Cleyn's design (fig. 63) into a bench on which to set forth another row of cooked foods. He apparently failed to read the text and so did not include the sturgeon and pickled salmon, which would have added variety to his drawing. But Hollar

63) CLEYN, from *Aesop Paraphras'd* (1651), 147 × 90 mm.

62) HOLLAR, from *Aesop Paraphras'd* (1665), 214 × 162 mm.

turns his illustration into a fine print by imagining strong early morning sunlight coming from the right to light up the grey forms of the servant and the food and whiten what would be the grey surfaces of the door, the floor, and the left wall. He repeats the same lighting effects in a similar larder scene for 'The Fox and the Weasel'.

If Hollar's understanding with Ogilby was that he improve Cleyn's illustrations, not create fresh interpretations of the paraphrases, then he was probably justified in leaving out most of Cleyn's additions to the traditional motifs, introduced in order to try to illustrate the paraphrases. But he faced a different decision when he used nine of Gheeraerts' designs for his models. As he began work on his first fable, 'The Cock and the Pretious Stone' (fig. 64), Hollar seems to have decided that Cleyn's efforts to follow Ogilby's text by combining a barnyard scene, scholars in an interior without a wall, a sunrise, and a frightened lion was both ludicrous and inelegant. He chose instead to follow Gheeraerts in making the cock examining the gem unmistakably the centre of interest and to omit the rest of the Ogilby references. He follows Cleyn only by including the 'wives, concubines, and fair race of the cock' to which Ogilby refers. Otherwise he is indifferent to the text. And when he substitutes a walled castle on a hill in the distance for Gheeraerts' village, in which a verger with a lantern precedes a priest with the Host to early Mass, he reveals his preference for the ornamental over the relevant.

Similarly in the second fable (fig. 65) Hollar dismisses Cleyn's effort to combine the traditional motif of a dog and his reflection with Ogilby's reference to beggars outside a mansion. He follows closely Gheeraerts' drawing of a dog on a plank over a stream with a gnarled tree beside it, but then for Gheeraerts' sleepy Flemish village beside the stream he substitutes an irrelevant French chateau with a mildly obtrusive drawbridge over a moat. Again he has sacrificed both Cleyn's loyalty to his author and Gheeraerts' unity of place for his own vision of a comely design. The vertical chateau towers on the left and six bare tree trunks on the right, plus their reflections in the water, and the horizontal plank, which he has shifted from the oblique, establish a structure of great clarity and serenity.

Ogilby's one addition to the 1651 collection of paraphrases, no. LXXXII, 'Of the Frogs Fearing the Sun Would Marry', is an explicit satire on the Dutch – the second Anglo-Dutch war began in 1665. He has the 'frogs' assemble in the Damm in Amsterdam before the new State-house (later the Royal Palace), which he ridicules because it was then adorned by statues of pagan gods and goddesses. For the first time Hollar is entirely alone with Ogilby's text. He does a sober drawing of the building and fills the Damm before it with frogs dressed as burghers. They listen to addresses by their leader on one side and Neptune on the other. The literal representation of the scene with frogs substituted for Dutch citizens is too matter-of-fact to be either amusing or distinguished.

* * * * *

64) HOLLAR, from *Aesop Paraphras'd,* 220 × 165 mm.

the Dog. and Shadow.

In order to complete the discussion of Hollar's interpretive illustrations, we shall go on to his part in a volume published by Ogilby in 1668. In that discussion there will be references to Barlow's *Aesop's Fables* of 1666, which we shall take up in the next chapter, together with his share in the 1668 volume.

Ogilby's Aesopics (*1668*)

In the westward reach of the Great Fire of 1666 Ogilby's house in King's Head Court burned with a loss amounting to £3,000. The printer Roycroft's shop was also destroyed. If Roycroft had tried to save any of Ogilby's sheets that he may have had on hand by transferring them to St. Faith's in the crypt of St. Paul's, as many printers did, they would also have been lost. Ogilby did save the plates of the 1665 *Aesop Paraphras'd*. In 1668 he fearlessly republished these verse paraphrases and added three new poetic works: *Aesopic's: or a Second Collection of Fables Paraphras'd in Verse, Androcleus*, and *The Ephesian Matron*. He is said to have written these works during the Plague as the guest of Robert Le Wright of the Middle Temple in his house at Kingston-on-Thames. The two hundred and thirty-one pages of these new works are numbered consecutively, but only *Aesopics* has a title-page. It also has a second copy of the portrait of the author by Lely originally engraved by Faithorne, this one attributed to him but engraved by an inferior hand. Ogilby always received excellent typography from Thomas Roycroft. In general appearance this 1668 Ogilby folio is one of the lordly volumes of British book-making. It is also an early example in England of illustrations making a work of literature memorable.

There are fifty new fables in *Aesopic's, or a Second Collection of Fables Paraphras'd in Verse*. (The apostrophe is probably there by mistaken analogy with 'Aesop's', but the running head for both *Aesop Paraphras'd* and *Aesopic's* in this edition is 'Aesops Fables' with no apostrophe.) *Aesopics* is used here to distinguish the two collections. Only forty-one of the fables are illustrated because sometimes several fables are about the same characters. The arithmetic of the plates and illustrations is a little confusing. There are thirty-eight new illustrations, and three of Hollar's 1665 plates are used again, a sign of some sort of difficulty. But there are only thirty-six new plates because two illustrate two fables apiece. It looks as though Hollar began to illustrate the entire collection in 1666, the only date he puts on a plate, but could not finish. At the last minute (*i.e.* in 1668) Barlow came in to lend his neighbour, rival, and friend Ogilby a hand. And Josiah English, a Mortlake amateur and pupil of Francis Cleyn, helped out with one plate. There is an F on the plate for 'The Bald Man and the Fly', but the etching is Hollar's.

65) HOLLAR, from *Aesop Paraphras'd*, 252 × 169 mm.

Of the nineteen new illustrations on eighteen plates that Hollar etched, ten are original. The sources for the rest, all previously mentioned Aesops, are diverse: Solis one, Gheeraerts two, Barlow four, Stoop one, and Hollar one. English etched and probably designed a plate, which he derived from one of Barlow's 1666 illustrations.

It seems safe to say that Barlow designed the remaining eighteen *Aesopics* illustrations on seventeen plates. The eight that Gaywood etched can be identified by comparison with the plate for Fable XIV signed 'F. Barlow inven. R. Gaywood fecit 1668'. Of the other plates, seven are unattractively engraved on six plates by an anonymous hand – a religious Englishman, to judge by his 'it came to pass' doodled in tiny letters on one plate, perhaps as he tested the sharpness of his burin. Then three are etched just as unattractively by another anonymous hand. Barlow probably drew these ten illustrations. A number of them include animals and birds, incidental details are like those in Barlow designs, and Barlow is the only likely candidate.

The distribution of sources of motifs used by Barlow is as wide as for Hollar: Zainer three, Gheeraerts two, Solis two, Barlow (1666) two, and Solis-Barlow one. The rest are original.

Thus, as we might expect, we have a nearly equal division of plates between Hollar and Barlow, with one by English. Of the new illustrations in *Aesopics* eighteen are original, and twenty borrow motifs in varying degrees, Barlow's *Aesop's Fables* being the inspiration for eight and part of another, perhaps a sign of pressure. In addition, three of Hollar's plates from *Aesop Paraphras'd* are pressed into service again.

Because ten of his designs are original and Cleyn no longer influences his thinking, Hollar's *Aesopics* illustrations seem more interesting than those in *Aesop Paraphras'd*, though, with one or two exceptions, they reflect little or no appreciation of Ogilby's satire. This freshness shows itself in various ways. The background of a farmhouse and a distant village church in 'The Ox and the Steer' (fig. 66) suggests that Hollar has noted the fitness of Barlow's English settings. The rhythmic arrangement of woodsmen in 'The Cedar and the Shrub' (fig. 67) creates one of Hollar's most original and dynamic interpretive illustrations.

Hollar adds expressiveness to several of his designs. In the illustration of 'The Dog in the Manger', the ox is patient, the dog is vicious, and the master angry. His original illustration for 'The Crammed Capons and the Lean One' (fig. 68) sums up the traditional fable. The richly gowned major domo comes out into the chicken yard and tells the maid that the capons, who have been stuffing themselves, must be killed for a banquet, all except the lean one, who has guessed what is going on. (Ogilby's moral, however, is that a short life and a merry one is

66) HOLLAR, from Ogilby: *Aesopics*, 255 × 189 mm.

67) HOLLAR, from *Aesopics*, 237 × 190 mm.

68) HOLLAR, from *Aesopics*, 241 × 194 mm.

69) HOLLAR, from *Aesopics*, 245 × 196 mm.

better than a long life whose 'business' is 'scarce worth one Potage'.) Similarly Hollar puts the whole of 'The Wind and the Earthen Vessel' into his design. The potter comes running out of his shop too late to save his braggart earthen jug from the jet-like blast of Boreas. He even loses his cap, a minor point in the text. Charles II came to agree with Ogilby's blunt advice that princes should not engage in foreign wars 'till they are settled in Kingdoms regained'.

Two of the *Aesopics* illustrations are triumphs of Hollar's technique. In 'The Swan and the Stork' (fig. 69) Ogilby satirizes both turncoats feathering their nests and the Restoration stage: the Dublin impresario of the '40s must have felt out of it in London in the roaring '60s. Hollar has to invent a fresh design. He takes his cue from Cleyn's design for 'The Fox and the Ape', which he had already redone (fig. 60), and dresses up his two fowl according to Ogilby's specifications. Then instead of having them meet on the Strand above the Thames, as they do in the text, he places them on the strand of an indefinite body of water, graced by three actual swans and a stately home, symbols of peace and privilege. As always, it is impossible to 'read' what Ogilby's characters are talking about, but the illustration makes clear that he is satirizing court types. The artist who created two fascinating series of prints merely by drawing women in the costumes of the day has no trouble in dressing up these birds so that they are at once deliciously absurd and captivating.

The most magnificent of all Hollar's interpretive illustrations is the one for 'The Crab and Her Mother' (fig. 70). This is another of the slight traditional fables without revealing action. The mother criticizes her offspring for walking sideways. After she tries to demonstrate how to do it properly, the daughter says, 'First learn yourself, and then your Daughter teach'. The motif of two crabs or crayfish had come down with little change from Pfister's 1461 edition. The pair are invariably shown side by side, either on the bank of a stream or, as in Gheeraerts' version, swimming in it, with little differentiation in size. Here Hollar's visual imagination conjures up a better concept.

Having a large plate and no accessories to include, he fills the entire lower half with a virtually scientific drawing of the two crabs, the unmistakably smaller daughter at right angles to the parent, their claws interlocked. They lie high on a beach overlooking the wide sweep of a harbour with ships at anchor off the port and tiny fishermen hauling in a net at the water's edge in the mid-distance, a bit of business borrowed from Gheeraerts' 'Eagle and the Snail', as, indeed the harbour with distant headlands is almost a Gheeraerts' property. The success of this design derives to a considerable degree from Hollar's adoption of Gheeraerts' principle of relating the fable actors to their environment, here one in which they belong, although never so far from water.

70) HOLLAR, from *Aesopics*, 238 × 190 mm.

But what makes Hollar's 'life' study so exciting is the sensory realization of the sculptured marvel of the crabs' shells and legs and claws, accentuated by being seen from above in strong light and shadow, the St. Catherine's wheel of their extended legs and claws perhaps suggesting with what energy the forces of nature spend themselves, remote and indifferent to the affairs of men, symbolized by the distant port. It is a wonderfully evocative illustration, but the idyllic feelings it evokes would never arise from reading Ogilby's acerbic satire.

In illustration after illustration through *Aesop Paraphras'd* and *Aesopics* Hollar stands outside the Aesopic tradition, or rather like Gheeraerts and Barlow he modifies it. Gheeraerts did it by encapsulating the fabulous events within his own provincial Flanders. What Barlow did, we have yet to see. Indifferent to the new demands of Ogilby's text, Hollar accepts the traditional motifs and takes as his prime responsibility the promise of the title-page, the adornment of the book, and that he fulfils, sometimes with a splendour rare in any English book. He is the first artist in England to aim at making book illustrations independent works of beauty.

Hollar's Ephesian Matron *Series*

The fourth work in Ogilby's 1668 folio is *The Ephesian Matron: or Widow's Tears*. Ogilby retells in tasteless couplets Petronius's *Satyricon* version of this macabre tale. The iron-willed widow of Ephesus saves her soldier lover by desecrating the corpse of her husband and substituting it on the gallows for the corpse of a male-factor stolen while the lover neglected his watch. The ten large etchings (*c.* 245 × 195 mm.) have the unusual virtue of uniformity. Two are dated 1666. By plan or otherwise, it looks as though of Ogilby's three new 1668 works Hollar and Barlow completed one apiece – the *Ephesian Matron* and *Androcleus* respectively – and divided the other, the *Aesopics*. It also seems that for some reason Hollar did not work on this volume after 1666. For an artist so brilliant and productive and able to etch his own designs, it is shocking to realize that *The Ephesian Matron* is Hollar's only exclusive monument as an original interpretive illustrator.

In these remarkable plates Hollar aims at effects quite different from those of the fables. Their restraint and lack of theatrical gesture contribute to the tension as the unholy events unfold, and Hollar's fondness for large areas of fine cross-hatching gives the chiaroscuro of the scenes an appropriate lithographic tonality. (The difficulties of the printer in coping with the technical problem of getting sharp impressions of these plates should not obscure their merits.)

The first illustration, printed as a frontispiece to the poem, is one of great elegance (fig. 71). A richly dressed couple walk hand in hand on a terrace above a

71) HOLLAR, from Ogilby: *The Ephesian Matron*, 236 × 189 mm.

sunken formal garden. Other couples strolling in the garden may be imagined as guests come for a wedding-anniversary feast. Filling the background are the high towers and round temple of the walled city of Ephesus, etched with Hollar's inimitable delicacy. He uses one of his favourite devices here: he throws a strong side light on the heavily etched foreground figures and then etches the background so lightly that the main actors stand out dark and three-dimensional while the city recedes.

The husband has a presentiment of death, he bids his wife be chaste, the plague seizes him, and he dies. In the second illustration a solemn funeral procession issues from the gateway of Ephesus, meticulously shown as the same city as in the first illustration, now seen closer and from a different angle. To show both the corpse borne uncovered on a bier and the widow and immediate mourners in the same plane, Hollar ingeniously picks the moment that the procession makes a right turn. On a hill in the midground a soldier guards another corpse hanging from a gibbet. Again Hollar gives weight to the dark figures in the foreground, the widow set apart by a white mourning wimple, and by light grey etching he makes the intricate temple and the massive crenellated walls and towers of Ephesus seem almost to float.

In the third illustration the Matron stands in the candle-lit tomb above her dead husband (she could hardly kneel, as the text requires) and with hand raised swears to be faithful.

Although it is spring, a storm of hail, rain, and snow 'the like not seen in many years before' drives the 'Martial' who has been guarding a hanged malefactor into the burial 'Lodge' in order to keep from freezing. Illustration IV shows a Roman soldier in a plumed helmet presenting himself to the Matron, while her maid stands quietly in the shadows beside a fireplace in this well-appointed mausoleum. In illustration V the widow compassionately shares her supper with the soldier, still wearing his helmet and the maid still passive in the shadows behind her. Illustration VI reveals the now amorous soldier pressing his attentions on the Matron, who threatens him with a knife as she retreats to where her husband lies.

Inexplicably, however, she smiles at the last moment, and the soldier pursues her. In illustration VII Ogilby covers the breaking of her vow by an interlude of his own invention, in which naked Venus and Cupid appear hand in hand on a cloud, and Venus gives the proceedings her ambiguous sanction.

Before dawn the soldier discovers that the body of the malefactor has been stolen from the gallows in order to give him a proper burial. As punishment, the soldier will have to take his place. In illustration VIII (fig. 72) the Matron, assisted by her lover and maid in the dark tomb, lops the right hand, ears, nose, and lips from the rigid body of her dead husband as the malefactor's have been. Then in

72) HOLLAR, from *The Ephesian Matron*, 251 × 200 mm.

illustration IX before day breaks the three hang the body of the husband in the chains of the gallows in place of the missing malefactor. The design is a reversal of the Deposition.

The partners in infamy fall out, but in illustration X Venus and Cupid reappear. Venus reports that husband and malefactor have been restored to their correct states and places, and she enjoins the once again loving pair kneeling before her to live happily together. They do.

Except for Ogilby's off-key Venus and Cupid interpolations, the murky scenes move along in a taut cinema-like progression. They give an uncanny impression of being overseen from a hidden vantage point, and the equivocal actions of the Matron, as revealed in the still etchings, strike the reader with a grim force not realized in the poem. It is an irony of English book illustration that in his only complete and original series Hollar should achieve a striking success not by his superb decorative draughtsmanship but by his ability to convey the dark and sinister mood of the events in the text.

The Octavo Aesop Paraphras'd *and* Aesopics (*1673*)

The burdens of his geographical enterprises did not stop Ogilby from publishing a 'second edition' of his *Aesop Paraphras'd* and his *Aesopics*, 'printed by the author, at his house in White-Friars' in 1673. It was actually the fourth for the *Aesop Paraphras'd*. To appeal to a wider market, he reduced his folios to a two-volume octavo. (They must have sold well because two years later T. Basset, R. Clavel, and R. Chiswel, using the same plates, presented a 'third edition' to be sold by Samuel Keble.) For this popular edition Ogilby had reduced copies (*c.* 45 × 95 mm.) of the 1665 and 1668 plates made by engraving and etching. Some are reversed and some are not. One engraver of the *Aesop Paraphras'd* plates signed nos. 57 and 58 with the initials 'R N', and the hand that adjusted faithfully to reproducing the oddities of Gaywood's versions of Barlow's *Androcleus* designs missed the one for section XIX. The etcher imitates Hollar well, especially his *Ephesian Matron* designs. In this edition Ogilby anticipated the small illustrated book that came to England from France in the eighteenth century, just as he had La Fontaine's and Gay's paraphrases of Aesop.

ÆSOP's
FABLES
With his Life
In English French & Latine.
The English by Tho. Philipott Esq.
The French and Latine
by Rob. Codrington M.A.
Illustrated with
one hundred and ten
SCULPTURES.
By Francis Barlow.
And
Are Sold at his House,
The Golden Eagle
In New-Street,
near Shoo-Lane.
1665

CHAPTER VIII

Barlow's
Aesop's Fables
(1666)

W E HAVE COMPLETED our survey of book illustration in England before 1700 and the Aesopic tradition as carried forward by Francis Barlow's predecessors Marcus Gheeraerts, Francis Cleyn, and Wenceslaus Hollar. We have also completed our account of the earlier work of Barlow. Now we can look without interruption at his chief work, his illustrations of *Aesop's Fables* (1666), and then at his later works – his contributions to John Ogilby's *Aesopics* (1668), his complete series for Ogilby's *Androcleus* in the same volume, and finally his Life of Aesop series for his own second edition of *Aesop's Fables* (1687).

Barlow the Publisher

It is natural that soon after the Restoration Francis Barlow should decide to illustrate an edition of *Aesop's Fables*. As we have seen, during the 1650s he was already recognized as the leading bird and animal artist of England, and his studies of birds and animals were described in Latin as by Francis Barlow, the distinguished English painter. In 1666, therefore, the year following the handsome Ogilby-Hollar edition of *The Fables of Aesop Paraphras'd in Verse,* Barlow also turned publisher and brought out his edition of the fables together with a life of Aesop not provided by Ogilby. William Godbid was the printer. Thomas Philipott prepared the English text and Robert Codrington the French and Latin.

Barlow planned publication for 1665. He etched an ornamental title-page (fig. 73) with that date engraved on the central cartouche. Publication ran over into the next year, for on the printed title-page the date is 1666. Evidently all of the etched-engraved title-pages for the edition had been printed, and it was too expensive to correct the date and print them again. The etched illustrations probably had been printed, too. They were not inserted like Hollar's but printed on the same pages as the Latin text with the French text of the next fable on the verso. The letterpress clearly overprints on the bottom of several plates. Since the type can be adjusted and the plates cannot, and the two cannot be printed on

73) BARLOW, from *Aesop's Fables,* 238 × 159 mm.

the same press, the etchings would be run off first. On the printed title-page the 'sculptures' were increased from a hundred and ten to a hundred and twelve by counting the frontispiece and the etched title-page. Between title-pages Barlow decided to turn the selling over to Ann Seile and Edward Powell. The Plague having driven potential buyers out of London may have discouraged him from emulating Ogilby as bookseller as well as publisher. Ann Seile was doubtless the widow of Henry Seile, one of the booksellers of *Theophila*, since on his death she took over his shop beside St. Dunstan's in Fleet Street. Powell had his shop at the White Swan, Little Britain. He was one of the sellers of Barlow's Devil and Egg political cartoon.

Frontispiece and Title-Page

Barlow's *Aesop's Fables* opens with a frontispiece facing an etched and engraved title. The frontispiece (194 × 155 mm.) is a complete re-doing of the traditional one followed by Cleyn and Hollar but not Gheeraerts. Aesop stands among his animal characters and a few birds, all beautifully drawn, their naturalness and gentleness exemplified by a ram snuffling Aesop's knee. (The unusual detail of a peacock in a tree shows that Barlow made use of Cleyn's version.) In Hollar's larger design a worried-looking Aesop addresses a group of sceptical men and one woman. The animals, also worried looking, are scattered about in a disorganized way. Characteristically, Barlow leaves out the cluster of human beings, so that he can draw with loving realism the animals in a wholly new grouping. Humble and mis-shapen, Aesop is no longer the hydrocephalic clown of Virgil Solis and other earlier illustrators, but a sensitive, thoughtful man, once a slave, now almost mystically at one with the speechless animals. Gheeraerts' title-page design was drawn to fit the biblical text of man's dominion over the creatures of the land, sea, and air. The vision that Barlow sees is in his heart, not in the text; yet in transcending his text he has created one of the magnificent pages in an English book.

The delightful facing title-page (fig. 73) is Barlow's own invention; even cold baroque ornamentation comes to life under his touch. The conventional oval cartouche, in which the title was too-early engraved, is supported by a genially unheraldic group. Holding up the corners, a bear and a bare-fanged boar crouch ready to defend the book against all readers. Clinging to the sides are a lion and a tiger, the lion uncomfortable because from above a magisterial eagle is scolding him. In centre stage at the bottom sits a bright little fox, looking as detached as a Swiss banker. Seldom has the design problem of filling the space around a baroque scroll been solved so ingeniously or with more vibrant life. At the threshold of one of the most eminent of English illustrated books, these two facing plates demonstrate Barlow's power without sentimentality to express his affection and respect for all manner of creatures and without artifice to reveal them in their beauty and dignity.

The British Museum has a fine large etching after Barlow of Orpheus seated beneath a tree playing a lute and surrounded by twenty-five animals and six birds (217 × 303 mm.). This variant of the frontispiece to Barlow's Aesop may have been suggested by Gheeraerts' title-page for *De warachtighe Fabulen der Dieren*, but it seems intended as a separate print, one of the later ones perhaps etched by Francis Place. Robert Peale sold it.

His Words to the Reader

The book is dedicated 'To the Honourable The great Fautor [patron] and Promoter of all ingenious Sciences in which Himself is so great a Proficient, Sir Francis Pruijan [*sic*]'. Along with some obsequious and highfalutin prose, Barlow plainly states his hope: 'If Aesop was acceptable to all, when in his native, rude, and home-spun habit; how much more now, being apparel'd in a variable dress and appearing in publique with the concomitant attendants of two Foreign Languages.' Prujean, the royal physician and amateur scientist, came from Lincolnshire, as we have noted, which lends some weight to the early statements that Barlow did, too. The doctor inconsiderately died on 23 June 1666.

In 'To the Reader' Barlow makes the only enlightening comments about illustrating by an English artist printed before 1700, unless Henry Peacham's remarks about emblem books in his *Minerva Britanna* [1612] be considered enlightening. Barlow genuinely takes the reader into his confidence. He addresses himself to the 'Courteous Reader, and those more curious [skilled] in their knowledg as to Design in Pictures'. He says that he was 'pressed into this great Work, some years since, by the perswasion of a much honoured Friend of mine (since dead)'. Thus he has been preparing the drawings over several years. The friend thought it would suit Barlow's fancy because it consisted 'so much of Fowl and Beasts, wherein my Friends are pleas'd to count me most Eminent'. Barlow says 'that it might be more useful for young Gentlemen and Ladies as well as others', he has 'with great charge and trouble' provided English, French, and Latin texts to improve their knowledge in those languages, 'which I hope may prove delightful'. Accordingly, he says, he has placed 'in every Opening, the Fable Pictures'. And he then casts some light on current illustration and on himself:

Now as there is no Garden but amongst many Flowers there may be some Weeds, so possibly some of my Designes may be questioned by the more Critical; or at least, not being Graven, all of them appearing not so pleasant to the Eye of many: truly I shall presume to beg this favour from you, first to consider I am no pro-fessed Graver or Eacher, but a Well-wisher to the Art of Painting; and therefore Designe is all we aim at, and cannot perform Curious [fastidious] Neatness with-out losing the Spirit, which is the main. And as in Garlands, Flowers together shew well; being severed, many may prove not so good: so I hope in the general I may in some measure answer your Expectation, which will be the Crown of my so great pains, and the happy Accomplishment of the desires of

Your Servant to command
F.B.

Barlow probably had reason to believe that his limited contemporary public would expect burin engravings in so expensive a book. But while he repeats what he had written to Evelyn ten years before, that he was not a professional etcher, his best work does not bear out this criticism, though it is not so fastidious as Hollar's. What he seems to mean is that painting is his main business and also that since he has to draw his illustrations on paper first, he finds the fussy process of transferring them to the plates and then etching them uncongenial.

The Polyglot Text

Thomas Philipott and Robert Codrington were industrious authors of miscel-laneous works and translations. Philipott, versifier of the fables in English, went from Somerset to Clare Hall, Cambridge and took his M.A. in 1635/36. His path touched Barlow's at several points. As mentioned before, he was given aid by Benlowes, to whom he addressed complimentary verse in *Theophila*. His *Villare Cantiarum* (1659), a book on Kent, actually written by his father, was printed by William Godbid, printer of Barlow's Aesop, and it contains a map on which are two etchings by Hollar. His *Historical Discourse of the First Invention of Navigation* (1661) was, like Barlow's Aesop, dedicated to Sir Francis Prujean. He also wrote *Self-Homicide-Murther* (1674), an echo of Denny's *Pelecanicidium*. He died in 1682. Codrington, responsible for the French and Latin versions of the fables, studied at Magdalen College and received his M.A. from Oxford in 1626. In 1641 he was imprisoned for writing an elegy on the Earl of Strafford but was later on the side of Parliament. His books include a life of Essex (1646) and translations of the *Heptameron* (1654) and a life of Alexander the Great (1661). His work for Barlow was his last; he died in the Plague.

For a person whose aberrant spelling and awkward syntax suggest little formal schooling, Barlow's polyglot approach is surprising. He must have known the dramatist-schoolmaster friend of John Ogilby, James Shirley, who was also his own neighbour. The inspiration for his pedagogical approach to Aesop may well have been the excellent one hundred and eighty-four-page English-Latin-Greek textbook, first printed in 1656, and fifty-six pages of parallel fables from Aesop which Shirley prepared for the pupils of his school in Whitefriars.

Godbid and Barlow turned out a neat folio that has its *raison d'etre* in the dominant appeal of the illustrations and the readers' familiarity with the essential stories of the fables. Still it is not exactly what the reader might expect. First comes the Life of Aesop, told three times over, in English (forty pages), French (thirty-one pages), and Latin (seventeen pages). In this edition it is not illustrated. Then on opened pages a fable and moral in French exactly fill the verso page, Codrington's moral often being two or three times longer than the fable. On the upper half of the recto are an illustration (*c.* 130 × 160 mm.) and engraved on the 35 mm. space beneath on the same plate Philipott's fable in three to six English couplets followed by the moral in one couplet. In the bottom half of the recto the fable and moral are set forth concisely in Latin. It is doubtful that the French and Latin texts justified the large amount of space they took up. In fact, the oddity of the edition is that the fables receive such short shrift in English. Philipott's couplets sum up the traditional fables briskly in phrases so rough-hewn that they can owe little literary debt to anyone, and the morals, though often fresh sounding, stick to universals with none of Ogilby's contemporary references.

The British Museum Aesop Drawings

Fortunately preserved in the Department of Prints and Drawings of the British Museum are a hundred and fourteen of Barlow's original drawings for the 1666 and 1687 editions of *Aesop's Fables,* and they have been individually described in Croft-Murray and Hulton's *Catalogue of British Drawings: XVI & XVII Centuries.* They include drawings for the '1665' title-page and eighty-four fables, plus two rejected variants. They were first made in blue-grey wash and then their outlines and details indicated with a pen or 'pencil' brush in sepia ink. They have every sign of being right the first time (fig. 74). With several exceptions they are painstakingly finished. The exceptions are bare; they tend to have low horizons and little background detail and to be in black lead and wash only. They look like early drafts that Barlow meant to redraw. The original drawings have been pasted at the corners on drawing paper and bound. It is possible, however, to see marks of tracing on parts of some drawings and black lead or red chalk on the

74) BARLOW, drawing for *Aesop's Fables*, 131 × 144 mm.

backs of most. Tracing marks are not apparent at all on many of the drawings and not all over on any one because Barlow traced them with such care that the mark of his hard stylus point registers only on some dark thick lines. (As mentioned in Chapter I, there are several ways to transfer a design to a plate.) Barlow took care not to damage the drawings over which he had taken such pains for so long.

Not one of the etched plates has a signature of any kind; yet so sensitively is the spirit of the drawings reflected in the plates that Barlow must be his own etcher. (Of course, the title-page and To the Reader leave no doubt that he is.) The etchings are almost mirror reflections of the drawings, though in a different medium. The finality of the drawings shows what Barlow meant about not being a professional etcher: he used etching for reproducing drawings and did not trust himself to use it freely for fresh creative effects. Yet over a score of the printed designs have improvements that only Barlow would be likely or able to make in the course of transferring the drawings to the plates. Most are additions of birds and small animals to enliven empty spaces. In other plates two steers replace a ladder in a barnyard, a lion turns his head responsively instead of looking straight ahead, Jove is re-drawn to be less stiff, and a 'clown' becomes, as he should be, a workingman and is moved off centre.

Three designs are completely redrawn. The first drawing of the young man who loved a cat made the young man look like a woman in a housedress. On the other hand the etching of 'The Satyre and the Clown' loses the point of the fable: the 'clown' seems staring at his broth, not blowing on it as he should be and does in the first drawing. A revised drawing is not in the collection; the change prob-

75) BARLOW, drawing for *Aesop's Fables*, 128 × 162 mm.

ably was made without one. Finally, in 'The Old Lyon' we can see what Barlow may have meant to do with the less finished drawings mentioned above had not, in all likelihood, time run out on him. The first drawing of an ass kicking an old lion is close to Gheeraerts' static design. In the second drawing the ass turns his head to watch as he kicks, and the animals are rearranged in a more dynamic composition (fig. 75), which we shall look at later. These last-minute improvements give insight into Barlow's instinct for what is significant in the function of illustration.

Sources of Motifs and Degrees of Indebtedness

Barlow's indebtedness to earlier editions of Aesop varies a great deal. Several of his illustrations are straight copies, though never facsimiles. In many more instances he uses traditional motifs with such freedom that his etchings are essentially fresh interpretations, often to the extent that it is difficult to say which of two or three possible sources he had in front of him. The eclectic nature of Barlow's use of traditional motifs from the sources discussed in Chapter III and the degrees of his indebtedness can be shown approximately by the following table:

	Probable	Certain	With changes	Some doubt	Total
Zainer	1		1		2
Salomon	1	1	1		3
Plantin	1				1
Solis	2	2	1	3	8
Gheeraerts	17	7	16	6	46
Cleyn	5	3	3	2	13
Gheeraerts & Janot	1				1
Gheeraerts & Solis	1	1			2
Gheeraerts & Cleyn	3			1	4
Cleyn & Salomon	1				1
Cleyn & Solis	1				1
Uncertain	1		2		3
	35	14	24	12	85
				Original	25
				Total	110

These assignments are based on careful comparisons of each of Barlow's illustrations with illustrations for the same fables, when present, in the earlier editions listed in Chapter III. While some error and uncertainty are inevitable, the essential truth becomes clear as it does in no other way. Barlow uses Gheeraerts' complete series of illustrations as his main source for forty-six designs, plus five in which he uses Gheeraerts and another source also. Only seven of the forty-six are so close to Gheeraerts that the borrowing is certain, and seventeen are probable. In sixteen instances, where Gheeraerts also seems the probable or certain source, there are significant changes, while in six the borrowing seems probable but is still open to some doubt. Barlow's use of Cleyn as sole source possibly thirteen times, plus six times in combination, seems surprising. Sometimes he turned to Cleyn because Gheeraerts had not illustrated the fable, and sometimes because in borrowing the motif it made no difference to him which he used. Similarly, Barlow used Solis chiefly for motifs of designs for fables not in Gheeraerts' collection. His other scattered borrowings are probably from late editions or close copies rather than from first editions. Clearly he had a wide acquaintance with illustrated books. Only a fifth of the twenty-five original designs are for fables not illustrated in any of the listed editions; in the other twenty illustrations Barlow invents his own motifs in preference to existing motifs.

Mutation of Motifs

Barlow seems to respect traditional motifs as part of a game, like writing sonnets, but he shapes them into essentially English images, and finally he invents twenty-five original concepts and treatments. The degree of his indebtedness in the rest of the designs is suggested by the table, but the question of originality is a complex matter not limited to the underlying motifs, important as they are. In the main Barlow has a Shakespearean way with his sources: his duty is not to invent new formulations but to transmute old ones in the chemistry of his imagination. His illustrations so restate the traditional patterns and charge them with fresh impulses that they become unquestionably his own creations. In this all-important respect he is the greatest of English Aesopic illustrators.

The mutations of the treatment of the illustration of the same fable can be exemplified by tracing the design for the fable called in Barlow's edition 'The Stag in the Ox-stall'.

In the fable a stag pursued by hunters finds temporary safety in hiding under a pile of hay in an ox-barn, but in doing so increases his danger, for he is soon discovered and captured by the master and his servant. The first occurrence of the

76) GHEERAERTS, from de Dene: *De warachtige Fabulen der Dieren*, 92 × 109 mm.

motif in a printed book is the woodcut in Zainer's *Vita Esopi et Fabulae* [*c.* 1476], where the stag is inside and two men are outside. Janot (1542) has a completely different concept: a farmer grapples the stag by his antlers and neck (fig. 28). Salomon (1547), as usual, follows Janot but here alters the concept by having the farmer use the more sensible method of restraining the animal by a pitchfork at its neck. Solis (1566), as almost always, redraws Salomon's design. In 1567 Gheeraerts' etching turns Solis' woodcut into a modern barn scene (fig. 76), but the motif is Salomon's as repeated by Solis. He fills his modest plate with action and authentic detail. A mean-looking churl with sturdy legs and a cocktail in his cap pins down the helpless animal with a pitchfork made from a pronged sapling. Two oxen feed at the left, and a patched door with a leather pull lets in light at the right and across the design.

In Cleyn's 1651 illustration the rustic stands looking left into space with hand outstretched as though declaiming, 'Is this a dagger which I see before me?' In the other hand he holds a pitchfork vertically. At the right the stag's head pokes out of a pile of hay too small to conceal its body. Cleyn has concealed his borrowing by changing Gheeraerts' design until it becomes almost meaningless. He does add a glimpse of the hunt outdoors with three hounds searching for the scent. Hollar in 1665 saw that Cleyn's travesty would never do. Superficially his design does not seem to resemble Gheeraerts'. Yet he skilfully copies Gheeraerts' farmer with a fork at the stag's throat without significant changes – he even repeats the farmer's slashed shoulder pieces. His main change is to add three farmhands running in at a wide door at the right. Gheeraerts anticipated him in the use of a strong side-light in the grey interior.

77) BARLOW, from *Aesop's Fables*. 127 × 157 mm.

Barlow re-creates the entire event (fig. 77). With a close look at Gheeraerts'
etching and somehow at Janot's little 1542 woodcut or a later copy, he throws
himself into the implausible situation. He draws a burly bare-headed farmer
(another head that helps identify the *Electra* Elizabeth as etched by Barlow)
grappling the terrified stag, now half out of the hay, its head focused against the
dark shadow of the farmer's body. The farmhand, a secondary figure partly out
of the picture on the right, presses the fork against the stag's highlighted throat.
Even from the rear Barlow's oxen are fine beasts (though one is a cow) as they
indifferently eat their hay. For further compositional interest he adds a vertical
bearing beam with a diagonal roof support to catch the light, and he throws a
broken wagon wheel, a little theatrically, on the floor. Out of doors the stag
runs – as it had been running earlier, pursued but free. Barlow creates a big
dramatic scene in the barn. Every detail of the illustration derives its justification
from the intensity of the emotion he himself calls forth from the fable. Yet the
motif is Janot's of 1542.

Barlow's Technique

Etching is not much used as a medium for illustration not only because the plates
do not wear well but also because the fine lines tend to clot, as they often do in
Hollar's Ogilby plates. The openness and strength of Barlow's etching keeps this
difficulty to a minimum. His lines have a hair-thin to brush-stroke fluidity denied
engravings and pen-and-ink drawings. Etching cannot exactly duplicate the
spontaneous movement of an original drawing or the soft effects of wash tones,
but Barlow used it superbly for precision of detail – the head of the eagle on the
title-page, for instance – and for simulating textures, especially the skin and fur of
animals and the feathers of birds. And casually sketched background items in his
drawings, such as a farmer ploughing or a hunt, may register as crisp little vignettes, as they do more often and interestingly in Gheeraerts' plates.

Paradoxically, Barlow strengthens the outlines of his main actors and foreground forms to an extent that counteracts the subtlety of effect that is a chief
attraction of an etching. But Barlow was not making etchings: he was making
illustrations. He was illustrating fables that were intended to be 'useful for young
Gentlemen and Ladies as well as for others', and therefore clarity of communica-
tion is foremost. That he succeeds can be seen by comparing the instantaneous
comprehensibility of his illustrations with the often slower impact of those by
other artists.

Certain details crop up in so many of Barlow's designs that they are almost mannerisms. He tends to draw hands gesturing with almost obsessive care to increase expressiveness. His men often wear box-toed shoes that are much too short. His animals have round dark highlighted eyes like marbles. To add a bit of interest to foregrounds, especially the corners, he introduces a crinkly-leafed plant (as does Hollar less often) and a brier. In many of his country scenes appears a gate with diagonal struts extending from the top of a hockey-stick shaped support on the hinge side in order to prevent sagging. Since this type of gate is common in Gheeraerts' illustrations, Barlow may have been familiar with the eastern counties of England settled by the Dutch and Flemish exiles, Lincolnshire, for instance.

A pervasive sense of variety is part of the appeal of Barlow's illustrations. To some extent this is a technical matter. Negatively, he avoids the flat-plane profiles and the repetition of postures that make much of the work of his predecessors seem static. Positively, he draws his characters, especially the animals, at all sorts of angles and many with heads turned, as can be seen in the reproductions. He can do this only because of years of life studies, for even he could not have had in his sketchbooks all the poses he needed. What a difference this almost automatic treatment of postures makes can be seen in his design for 'The Wolf and the Lamb' (fig. 78). Usually this is one of the least enlightening of Aesopic illustrations – just two animals beside a stream, the lamb sometimes drinking. (Although the lamb is drinking downstream, the wolf insists it is muddying the water for him: the strong can take offence at the weak whether or not they have good reason.) Barlow places the lamb on the left side of a rivulet, facing forward, its pretty head turned to drink. The churlish wolf stands above on the other side and in the plane behind the lamb, snarling at the inoffensive creature.

By these related devices of turning bodies of chief actors out of a horizontal plane and placing two or more in retreating planes, Barlow secures a considerable sense of depth in the immediate foreground, as for instance in the frontispiece. This feeling of palpable depth, of space occupied vitally, is enormously enhanced by the sense of volume that Barlow habitually achieves through his shrewd modelling of forms as he moves a strong light around them.

In all probability Barlow's art studies fell far short of Gheeraerts', Cleyn's, and Hollar's. Yet in the academic fundamentals of anatomy and composition his designs seem superior to theirs. In *Aesop's Fables* he has less opportunity to reveal his mastery of the anatomy of human beings than of animals, but the figures of the rigidly dead man in 'The Belly and Members' and the satyr in 'The Satyre and Clown' have the competence he had already proved in *Theophila*. That Barlow's knowledge of animal anatomy surpasses that of most other English book illustrators is manifest throughout the reproductions in this book.

78) BARLOW, from *Aesop's Fables*, 129 × 163 mm.

How skilfully Barlow can re-compose a traditional motif so that it becomes melodious can be seen in his handling of 'The Old Lyon', one of the designs for which we noted that there are two drawings extant. The usual illustration of the fable of the humiliation that comes to the once powerful when they grow old and infirm shows a confusing group of animals around a horse kicking a recumbent lion. Barlow heightens the humiliation by substituting an ass for a horse. Then in the second drawing he reorganizes the animals. He masses three horned beasts

79) BARLOW, from *Aesop's Fables*, (detail).

of different heights – a goat, a bull, and a stag – on the left above the lion. He tilts the ass diagonally up the middle of the design so that its heels and the lion's head are off centre. Now the ass's head in the second drawing (fig. 75) is turned to look at the lion and lines up on the right between the similar shaggy heads of the horse above and the boar below. By making a frame of the onlooking animals at the sides, he clarifies the action and has room to give the ass the star role and to make him such a handsome fellow that he cannot be a villain.

Barlow's Animals and Birds

The special glory of the Aesop illustrations is Barlow's drawing of animals and birds. Gheeraerts was his master in presenting the creatures as realistically as possible in the actions called for by the fables but in the everyday surroundings that his imagination deemed appropriate. This was a long advance on the elegant simplicity of the woodcuts of Salomon and Solis and, happily, a long time before the demeaning anthropomorphism of the nineteenth century. But Barlow lived a century after Gheeraerts, in the age of the Royal Society; indeed, as we have seen, his animals and birds were of interest to some of the founders. In spirit he

80) BARLOW, from *Aesop's Fables*, 124 × 157 mm.

is more scientist than realist, more concerned with how his creatures are than how they seem. Studiously he records underlying bone structure and the stretch of covering muscles, the way fur lies and wings and feathers are attached, beaks curl and claws clutch, characteristic postures and expressions, and all of the precise factual data that are the starting points of scientific observation. He does this with common creatures like the toads in 'The Oxe and the Toad' (fig. 79) [detail] and 'The Porcupine and Adders' (fig. 80), and he does it, as if with a telephoto lens camera, with creatures like beavers, eagles, and kites that he probably did not study at close range. Even the dragon in 'The Viper and the File' (fig. 81) seems zoologically faultless.

81) BARLOW, from *Aesop's Fables*, 130 × 161 mm.

82) BARLOW, from *Aesop's Fables*, 128 × 155 mm.

It has been said more than once that Barlow's lions look somewhat heraldic.
They do, but they do not have the slightly comic human features that Hollar
gives them. Usually Barlow endows all the big cats with the power and grace of
his leopard in 'The Leopard and the Fox' (fig. 82). He must have studied the
lions in the Tower of London and other wild animals and birds from foreign
lands that were on show in London taverns and at country estates, but he could
not or at least did not devote to them the scrutiny he gave to the wild and domes-

83) BARLOW, from *Aesop's Fables*, 128 × 162 mm.

tic animals and birds of England. No artist has responded with more sensitivity
and less sentimentality to the gentle grace of deer, for instance, than Barlow does
in 'The Stag Looking into Water' (fig. 83) and 'The Old Deer and Fawn'. The
least of creatures, the frog, the hare, the snake, and the swallow, and the least
favoured of them, the ass, the boar, and the wolf – he draws them all with an
intimacy, charm, and inviolable integrity never surpassed in an English book,
never by Thomas Bewick, for instance.

185

84) Barlow, from *Aesop's Fables*, 129 × 163 mm.

85) ANON, from Steinhowel: *Vita Esopi et Fabulae* (Johann Zainer c. 1476), 75 × 110 mm.

From Gheeraerts Barlow derived a sense of environment, the idea that, as far as fabulous creatures can, his characters must seem to belong to a particular locale and way of life. We could wish that Barlow had followed Gheeraerts with more zeal in giving realistic midground glimpses of village and country scenes and had not filled in so many backgrounds with indeterminate hills, trees, and an occasional tower in order to get something high enough to be seen. But his foreground settings are English. In 'The Cock and the Precious Stone' (fig. 84) Barlow takes over a motif which had not changed since Zainer's woodcut (fig. 85) and makes it not only his own but also wholly English. For the first time from Zainer to Hollar the cock is not in profile, and the hens and chicks that Cleyn had added are shown in more varied elevations and in a circle about their lord on his dunghill examining a lost pendant instead of the symbolic prism of previous designs. Then Barlow adds a beldame in the window of the farmhouse, a farmhand in the door of the barn, and two pair of boars yoked to prevent straying, a crowded design but one of some historical value.

86) BARLOW, from *Aesop's Fables*, 124 × 159 mm.

The illustrations for 'The Fox and the Cock', 'The Old Woman and Her Maids', 'The Cat and the Cock', 'The Fighting Cocks and the Partridge', 'The Man and His Goose' (fig. 86), and 'The Doves, Kite, and Sparhawk' also give views of English farmyards. We have already suggested that the hockey-stick gate may show acquaintance with the eastern counties. The background village, with a windmill on an island-like hummock, in the other 'Doves and Sparhawk'

87) BARLOW, from *Aesop's Fables*, 128 × 160 mm.

illustration seems of the fen country. The deer illustrations (fig. 83) and 'The Old Hound' have relevant hunting scenes in the background. And in his illustrations for 'The Ringdove and the Fowler' (fig. 87) and 'The Angler and the Little Fish' (fig. 88) Barlow also blends fable illustration with a record of British sport, another dimension.

88) BARLOW, from *Aesop's Fables*, 125 × 153 mm.

The Master of Involvement

One of Barlow's conspicuous advances in Aesopic illustration is his habit of projecting his characters in action. He arrests birds and animals in motion that one would think only a highspeed camera could catch, as in 'The Birds, Beasts, and Bat' (fig. 89). In the midst of this furore, with the bat waiting to come down on the side of the winner, Barlow delightfully shows the little creatures at the bottom of the design, the cock, porcupine, spaniel, and cat, contributing mightily to the

89) BARLOW, from *Aesop's Fables*, 132 × 158 mm.

violence. Barlow borrows the motif for 'The Shepherd Boy and the Wolf' (fig. 90) from Gheeraerts. But his wolf not only runs more realistically; instead of grasping the sheep by the back of the neck, he grips it cruelly by the throat as he carries it upside down on its back so that its legs stick hysterically up in the air. The shepherd boy, hands outstretched, pursues ineffectually, and Barlow remedies a Gheeraerts' omission by adding a barking dog that bothers the wolf more than the boy does.

191

90) BARLOW, from *Aesop's Fables*, 126 × 162 mm.

Barlow's originality as an interpretive illustrator grows out of something more than his superb draughtsmanship. The constant emotional involvement of his characters, human and dumb creatures, in the scenes they act out so vigorously invests his illustrations with dramatic excitement almost totally lacking in Aesopic illustrations before. The customary design for 'The Countryman and Snake' has a man alone in a kitchen, axe raised, about to strike a snake which, revived by the

91) BARLOW, from *Aesop's Fables*, 128 × 162 mm.

warmth of the fire, is ungratefully about to attack the farmer, who has saved it from freezing. Barlow enriches the fable by imagining the reality – the farmer would have a family. Thus he shows the snake about to attack the farmer's wife, who shields a little girl, while a little boy sprawls in terror on the floor at the feet of the enraged farmer (fig. 91) holding a pitchfork. Total involvement.

Illustrating the fable of the vixen who revenges herself on the eagle that carries

193

off her cub by burning down the eagle's nest with the eaglets in it presents a problem. From the beginning of printing the vixen is shown setting fire to straw at the foot of the tree in which the eagle has its nest. The figures are small because the whole tree has to be included. In his illustration for 'The Eagle's Nest' (fig. 92) Barlow shows the vixen with her brand on a branch of the tree just below the nest. (Philipott's version of the fable has the threat of burning enough to secure the return of the cub.) This solution enables Barlow to use the full breadth of the

92) BARLOW, from *Aesop's Fables*, 129 × 164 mm.

plate to draw one of his most dramatic designs – the eagle close up, wings spread in full majesty, the cub in her beak, her eaglets crying hungrily. That leaves room to show the worried vixen, brand in mouth, ready to set fire to the aerie. (If a fox can build a fire, it can surely climb a tree.)

How his feeling for intensifying the drama implicit in the fables leads Barlow sometimes to create completely fresh designs can be seen in his illustration for 'The Captive Trumpeter' (fig. 93). This is one of the motifs that starts life as a

93) BARLOW, from *Aesop's Fables*, 126 × 160 mm.

woodcut in the first emblem book, Steyner's edition of Alciati (1531). The traditional motif shows the trumpeter on foot seized by two foot soldiers. Barlow finds this too tame and unrevealing. He mounts the three figures on horses and shows the frightened trumpeter turning his head from his forward-thrust trumpet to plead (unsuccessfully) for his captors to spare his life because he has not borne arms against them. One captor threatens him with a lance, while the other stretches his arms out to seize him. Dimly in the background a battle acts out the crime of all 'trumpeters', the men who incite others to kill. By a simple act of imagination, Barlow invents a dynamic alternative to a perfunctory motif.

Emotional involvement is at the heart of Barlow's success as an interpretive illustrator. His birds and animals, no less than his human beings, are the believable, reacting embodiments of those vain, gullible, shrewd, and predatory creatures that the legendary Aesop made immortal with the barest introduction – 'Once a cock met a fox', 'A young shepherd was fond of crying wolf'. Precisely because he treats Aesop's characters with such scrupulous respect, he is able to involve them in the action, not just put them on the stage. The difference is crucial in illustration. That is why his illustrations glow with 'Spirit, which', as he said, 'is the main'.

CHAPTER IX

Barlow's Designs for Ogilby's *Aesopics* and *Androcleus* (1668); his Life of Aesop Series (1687)

IN CHAPTER VII we saw that when Hollar was apparently unable to cope with the three substantial works that Ogilby added to *Aesop Paraphras'd* (1665) when he reissued that collection in 1668, Barlow lent a neighbourly hand to complete the job. Because he etched none of the *Aesopics* plates and anonymous hands prepared six of the plates, it is not obvious whether or not Barlow drew all of the designs, except one by Josiah English, that Hollar did not do. Yet it seems reasonable to think that he did. For instance, 'The Eagle and Other Birds', a crowned eagle surrounded by armed accipiters glaring down from a plinth on a gathering of defenceless fowl, a harsh satire of King Charles, could hardly have been drawn at this time by anyone but Barlow.

Luckily on the first plate by Barlow in the *Aesopics* his friend Gaywood took it into his head to sign 'F. Barlow inven. R. Gaywood fecit' (fig. 94). Since this is the only plate besides those by Hollar and English that is signed, it is the key to all of those etched by Gaywood and presumably designed by Barlow, not only in the *Aesopics* but also in *Androcleus*, the third work by Ogilby in this volume. This signed illustration has the traditional motif for 'The Lyon and the Kid', with the goat safely up on a cliff rejecting the blandishments of the lion below. Here Gaywood is at his best. Though he falls short of doing justice to Barlow's animals, here they are recognizable as Barlow's.

Another two of the Barlow–Gaywood illustrations deserve mention. In the one for 'The Rustick and the Flea' (fig. 95) the pitcher on the round table, the faces and costumes of the women, and the poplar trees so closely resemble those in the dinner scene in *Androcleus* (fig. 96) that there can be no question that Barlow and Gaywood worked together on *Androcleus*. Then Ogilby in 'The Fox and the Eagle' elected to retell without satire the fable of the vixen who recovered her offspring by setting fire to the eagle's nest. Barlow could not think of a motif any better than his own in the 1666 *Fables* (fig. 92). So he made a new drawing,

F. Barlow *inven.*   R. Gaywood *fecit.* 1658

94) B<small>ARLOW</small>, from Ogilby: *Aesopics*, 250 × 182 mm.

Fab: 31

95) BARLOW, from *Aesopics*, 249 × 181 mm.

An: Sect: 22:

96) BARLOW, from Ogilby: *Androcleus*, 250 × 182 mm.

97) Barlow, drawing for *Aesopics*, 250 × 181 mm.

which is in the Ashmolean Museum collection (fig. 97), with a slight rearrangement of the main elements and the addition of other incidents in the background. Gaywood here does pretty well in making an etching from Barlow's drawing and yet loses much of the authority and feeling that Barlow puts into his virtually identical plate.

Barlow's Designs for Ogilby's Androcleus (1668)

The next work in this 1668 volume is Ogilby's verse narrative, *Androcleus, or the Roman Slave*, an uncertain blend of bestiary satire and tall story first told by Aulus Gellius and more recently by George Bernard Shaw. Although none of the eighteen plates is signed in any way, Barlow drew thirteen of the full-page illustrations (*c.* 253 × 187 mm.), as a comparison with signed plate XIV in *Aesopics* and the signed frontispiece to Howell's *Parley of Beasts* makes evident. Of these Gaywood just as evidently etched twelve, and two anonymous hands etched and engraved the other. An anonymous hand engraved further plates, of which two are appropriate but unaccountably small. Whether or not Barlow had anything to do with these five plates is not clear. It would seem likely that he would draw the three full-page designs, but even more likely that he would not do the small plates, though both have animals in them.

Since Ogilby's *Androcleus* is a new version of the old tale, Barlow's illustrations are fresh inventions. We can see how he goes about his task of interpretation uninfluenced by precedent. Although Ogilby is both author and publisher, he seems to have given Barlow a free hand in the choice of scenes to illustrate and the way of illustrating them. Because Ogilby mixes satire of the Restoration court with a clumsy rehearsal technique, whereby almost the entire poem moves jerkily by characters telling what happened to them in the past, Barlow might have profited by advice.

In the first illustration, obviously enough, Androcleus, the only survivor of a shipwreck on the coast of Libya (sketched in the background in the old-fashioned way Barlow used in some of the *Aesopics* illustrations), removes a thorn from a lion's paw in a cave. Androcleus asks for food. In plate II the lion, the king of the beasts of Libya, calls them together. Ogilby's words reflect King Charles II's relations with Parliament, but Barlow sticks to the animal fable and shows the beasts from the rear in a circle beneath the lion as he harangues them, a design much like the frontispiece to Howell's *Parley of Beasts* (fig. 40). In the background the lion is shown subsequently attacking his subjects. This speech scene gives Barlow a chance to draw animals. It is not a vital incident, and its inclusion supports the idea that Ogilby had little to do with the illustrations.

98) BARLOW, from *Androcleus*, 250 × 181 mm.

An: Sect: 15:

In plate III the grateful lion king and his leading courtiers entertain the hungry Androcleus at a feast that turns his stomach. Ogilby satirizes the Restoration favourites, but again Barlow quite properly decides he can illustrate nothing but the ostensible narrative, far-fetched as it becomes in literal visual terms. He picks the transitional moment when an ape waiter, once human, serves Androcleus human food and wins his freedom. The ape recounts his past, including an escapade which an anonymous hand engraves as small plate IV, the ape dallying with his mistress as her husband enters.

It is, as we have said, hard to believe that Ogilby would engage a second artist to interrupt Barlow's series of drawings just to make two drawings, and it is even more puzzling, and depressing, that he should violate the harmony of the series by using two incongruously small plates. But this plate must be given its place as the first sophisticated English illustration of a scene common in Restoration drama and eighteenth-century novels, with a picaresque hero in place of the ape.

Next the lion, once King Amasis of Egypt, tells his story. Three of the five illustrations give Barlow appropriate opportunities to draw more animals, including the lion's meeting with Apollonius, who understands the speech of animals (fig. 98). The fifth shows a cat seated at table with high-born Egyptians while the lion, adopted as an object of worship by the people he used to rule, is humiliated by being played with by children.

Androcleus now tells the lion and dinner guests *his* story. The first illustration shows him as a little boy tugging at his father to get him away from a round table at which he and six other men stand playing at dice. That Androcleus' father loses all his money and in the next illustration Androcleus is driven to begging suggests some truth in the story that Ogilby's father's imprisonment for debt came about through gambling. The next four illustrations picture episodes after Androcleus joins the service of a Roman consul as a slave. First the consul's wife takes a fancy to Androcleus as he works out of doors. Next he dines luxuriously with the lady at an extraordinary round table (fig. 96), a scene similar to ones by Barlow in the Juvenal, *Aesopics*, and Life of Aesop. This scene is followed by one in which Androcleus tears himself away from the consul's wife in her ornate alcoved bed. The full-page plate is engraved, presumably by the same hand as the small ape-and-mistress scene. Androcleus is thrown in prison, from which he is rescued by his fiancée, the steward's daughter, with her father's key (fig. 99). A realistic illustration of a shipwreck brings Androcleus' rehearsal back to where the whole narrative began.

The society of animals palling on him, Androcleus makes his way to Carthage where he is recognized, captured, and shipped back to Rome. The devoted lion,

99) BARLOW, from *Androcleus*, 254 × 188 mm.

having followed him, is also captured and sent as a gift to the emperor in Rome. The last plate shows the standard joyful reunion of Androcleus and the lion. According to Ogilby, it occurs in the customary amphitheatre. Barlow presents them (Androcleus quaintly prepared to punch the hungry beast) on a round stage with groundlings standing before the curved boxes of the emperor and empress while the gentry look down from the gallery. That Barlow should take so playful a liberty with the text contributes further to the assumption that he and Ogilby were friends. Why Barlow felt any need to digress in this manner and where he got his model are unanswered questions. This plate is one of those etched by someone besides Gaywood, except for the figure of Androcleus, which is engraved.

Lacking the high seriousness of the *Theophila* designs, the traditional appeal of the *Fables* designs, and the virtue of their execution as etchings by Barlow himself, the *Androcleus* illustrations inevitably lack their distinction. Nor do they compare in style or emotional effects with Hollar's *Ephesian Matron* series. With the poorly etched and engraved plates and apparently no extant drawings to guide us, we cannot fairly judge the acuteness of Barlow's interpretations. We can be sure that his draughtsmanship, especially of animals, was as striking as ever, although he skimped some of the unfamiliar backgrounds. But probably Barlow could not bring off the feat of imagination that had infused his illustrations of *Theophila* with more piety than Benlowes' poetry. In *Androcleus* he seems not to have commanded the visual wit necessary to give Ogilby's faltering verse a similar lift. But we can say that these *Androcleus* designs, at least the ones with human actors, are the first of a long line of English illustrations picturing the non-heroic exploits of the leading characters in novels such as *Tom Jones, Roderick Random*, and *A Sentimental Journey*.

The Second Edition of Aesop's Fables (*1687*)

Twenty-one years after his 1666 edition of *Aesop's Fables* Barlow brought out a second edition. Apart from thinking that the times were now right for the book, Barlow must have had a long-standing desire to gain for his chief work the recognition and reward lost if, as seems probable, much of his stock burned in the Great Fire. Preserving his drawings and copper-plates was relatively easy. He continued as publisher with the notorious Henry Hills, Jr. as printer. Christopher Wilkinson, who succeeded Ann Seile 'at the Black-boy against St. Dunstan's Church in Fleet-street, Tho. Fox in Westminster-hall, and Henry Faithorne at the Rose in St. Paul's Church-yard' are now his booksellers. Faithorne was bookseller to the Royal Society.

Barlow makes several interesting changes in his new edition. He no longer feels it necessary to solicit approval of his use of etchings. 'To the Reader' now states tersely that the present edition has been improved by correction of the Latin text, 'a more Exact Translation from the Latest and Best French Edition', and thirty-one new 'Copper Plates' have been added to illustrate the life of Aesop. And he adds: 'The Ingenious Mrs. A. Behn has been so obliging as to perform the English Poetry, which in short comprehends the Sense of the Fable and Moral: Whereof to say much were needless, since it may sufficiently recommend it self to all Persons of Understanding'. Now at the end of her career the intrepid Aphra Behn (1640–1689), first professional English woman novelist and play-wright, may have smiled wryly at this ineloquence. Further evidence of Barlow's greater sense of security can be read in the manly dedication to the Earl of Devonshire that takes the place of the 'prostratedly devoted' one in 1666 to Sir Francis Prujean. (These notes are based on the Chatsworth copy of the 1687 edition in a contemporary gold-tooled binding executed for presentation by Barlow to the Earl, which is now at the British Library.) Barlow explains to the Earl that the fables contain 'the substance of a moral philosophy' that will serve as a guide to the conduct of life. He concludes by saying that he has endeavoured to render the work 'more Agreable, by the Additional Ornaments of Sculpture and Poetry' and that he is 'Ambitious of giving this Public Testimony of Your Lordships many Favours towards me'.

The changes in the 1687 edition led to changes in the two title-pages, the etched and engraved one (fig. 73) and the printed one. On the first Barlow burnished out the engraved text in the oval panel. Traces of the original letters can still be seen. In this area he had fresh copy engraved. He drops the references to Philipott and Codrington and to his address and gives the space to his own efforts: 'Illustrated with One hundred and twelve Sculptures; To this Edition are likewise added Thirty one Folio Plates Representing his Life by Francis Barlow'. 'Illustrated' in our sense has become established usage, and the size of the illus-trations is a sales feature.

Aphra Behn's Contribution

Barlow probably called on Aphra Behn in the first place because the Life of Aesop plates had to be inserted together between the English and French bi-ographies and could not, therefore, be easily related to the text by the reader. Mrs. Behn wrote two couplets that were engraved within a cartouche at the bottom of each plate. At first she tried to sum up the relevant incident in Aesop's life, but

she soon shifted to writing what are in effect 'morals'. Having engaged the celebrated lady for this task, Barlow decided to substitute her crisper, more sophisticated verse for Philipott's knotty English verse summaries of the fables in the
first edition. This was good publishing practice. Not only was Aphra Behn one of
the best-known writers in England; she wrote in the manner of the times. The
tone of her 'Moralls', however, is censorious rather than cynical, as in her version
of 'The Cock and the Gem':

> *A Cock who to a neighbouring Dunghill tries,*
> *Finding a gemme that 'mongst the Rubish lyes,*
> *Cry'd he – a Barly corne would please me more,*
> *Then all the Treasures on the eastern shore.*
> > *Morall*
> *Gay nonsense does the noysy fopling please,*
> *Beyond the noblest Arts and Sciences.*

The substitution raised a more elaborate problem than that of the engraved
title. Philipott's versified condensation of each fable, usually in five couplets, and
a one-couplet moral were engraved at the bottom of the same plate as each
illustration. Now on all the plates this area had also to be burnished down to
accommodate Mrs. Behn's two-couplet fables and one-couplet moral. The workman doing the burnishing feared damaging the bottom border of the design
above the verse: in many plates traces of the tops of the letters in Philipott's top
lines remain. In a few instances a small new plate for the new verse had to be inserted. Otherwise the plates for the fable illustrations are as fresh in 1687 as they
were in 1666.

Through error, in 1666 at Fable XVI the plate containing the illustration and
English verse for 'The Parliament of Birds' (pheasant, pye, etc.) was printed with
the French and Latin text for 'The Doves and Hawk'. Then at Fable CIV, when
the printer Godbid discovered his error, he ran 'The Doves and Hawk' plate and
repeated the French and Latin text in abridged form. In 1687 the correct plate
goes with the text for XVI, and the correct French and Latin text goes with 'The
Parliament of Birds' plate, with an alternative but correct title of 'The Peacock
and Pie' [pye].

The Traditional Motifs

The traditional description makes Aesop a heavy-headed humpbacked, pot-
bellied, stammering Phrygian slave, who earned his freedom and the adjective
'subtill' by his edifying fables. The prototype woodcuts of the Ulm frontispiece

and life sequence show most of these characteristics in moderation. After he becomes a freeman, the Ulm life sequence gives him dignity along with a gown and cap. Later versions are often retrogressive; Virgil Solis makes him close to a figure of fun. Gheeraerts and Barlow have characteristic reservations about using this image of Aesop. Gheeraerts did not have in his edition a life to illustrate, and instead of an Aesop frontispiece he substituted on the title-page the figure of an Orphic man with symbols of his biblical dominance over birds, beasts, and fish.

The source of the motifs for Barlow's Life of Aesop series seems to have been an edition from which the Life illustrations of both Jerome de Marnef's *Aesopi Phrygis Fabulae* (Paris, 1585) and Christopher Plantin's *Les Fables et la Vie d'Esope* (Antwerp, 1593) are derived. The natural source for both, as it was for their *Fables* illustrations, would be a series by Bernard Salomon for Jean de Tournes of Lyon, but I have not seen a Life of Aesop series by Salomon. Barlow's few deviations from the motifs in both De Marnef's woodcuts and the suave little etchings by Pieter van der Borcht in Plantin's series are definite enough to prove that he had another set before him, but the correspondences are so comprehensive that it is of academic interest only what that actual source is. The truth is that, to a greater degree than in his use of Gheeraerts' designs for the fables, Barlow uses the sources for his Life designs only as starting points for his own complex imaginings (fig. 100).

'Thomas Dudley fecit'

Barlow etched five unsigned plates (I, II, III, XVI, and XXXI) (not XXIX as Sparrow says) and Thomas Dudley, 'quondam condicipulus W. Hollar', as he states on plate XV, etched the twenty-six remaining. Dudley signs the majority of his plates with his name and 'fecit', which might well have been the warrant for attributing the invention of all of the designs to him, if we had not Barlow's drawings to tell us the truth. He also dates two plates 1678 and 1679, evidence of how long Barlow had been planning the second edition and a reminder of how unpredictable the facts of publishing can be. In his plates Barlow's etching is looser, less patient than it was in 1666. It looks as though he had grown bored with the 'curious' craft of etching after doing these plates and had turned the job over to Dudley. That he is indeed the etcher of the five plates indicated can be seen by a comparison of the faces and figures with those in the *Fables*, as, for example, the man vomiting at the right of the first illustration (fig. 101) and the man in 'The Man and His Goose' (fig. 102) in the *Fables*. Plate XVI differs enough from the drawing in the British Museum to suggest that for some reason Barlow

101) BARLOW, *The Life of Aesop,* from *Aesop's Fables,* (1687), 194 × 163 mm.

100) BARLOW, from *Aesop's Fables,* (1687), 220 × 175 mm.

did Dudley's plate over. He seems to have added no. XXXI, the last illustration, long after Dudley had finished the series. While it shows worshippers before a statue of Aesop, Mrs. Behn's verse refers only to 'thy sacred name great Charles'. The King had died in 1685. The difference between Barlow's own etching of his designs and Dudley's is not great enough either to destroy the integrity of his illustrations or to introduce a discordant new style. Dudley was a much more satisfactory translator of Barlow's designs than Gaywood. His technique resembles his master Hollar's only in its tightness and close cross-hatching. (The two-tone effects in a few plates, such as no. XXII, probably result from correcting weak impressions.) Although Dudley's traced reproductions of Barlow's drawings lack spontaneity, they are extremely faithful.

The Life of Aesop Illustrations

The thirty-one illustrations for Aesop's life (*c.* 240 × 162 mm.) are rich in baroque elaboration. Cunning architectural detail, ornate apparel, fantastic chairs and thrones, liliaceous trumpets, art nouveau goblets and wine pitchers, all evoke a credible world of artifice that would have delighted Aubrey Beardsley. And yet the stubby humped figure of Aesop, with his massive head, is a compellingly natural

102) BARLOW, from *Aesop's Fables*, (detail).

103) BARLOW, from *Aesop's Fables*, 129 × 163 mm.

centre of the eventful scenes from the beginning of his career as a slave, through his triumphs as counsellor of the mighty, to his last speech to the Delphians. In ten of the plates Barlow characteristically introduces a nondescript dog, perhaps his own. The several figures and their immediate surroundings fill most of the designs so completely that they are seen as actors on a stage. Drawn a dozen years or so after the smaller designs for the *Fables*, these powerful illustrations are worthy contributions to the immortality of the wise Aesop.

104) BARLOW, *The Life of Aesop*, 194 × 163 mm.

Aphra Behn's four lines of verse moralizing on each episode in Aesop's life are engraved within an ornamental border that is part of each plate. Lavishly, Barlow invents a different border each time, squeezing owls, dogs, snakes, gargoyles, fish, apes, and all manner of creatures within the 8–10 mm. space.

At first glance the Life of Aesop designs bear little resemblance to the *Fables* illustrations. They are twice as tall, and they deal exclusively with human beings, chiefly of the upper class. However, two or three of the *Fables* designs – 'The Lion in Love' (fig. 103) and 'The Young Man and His Cat', especially – contain similarly costumed figures and use similar architectural units in the foreground setting. And plate IV of the Life series, Aesop with a basket of fowl in a farmyard, is much like an illustration for the *Fables*. Barlow did not invent a new style for the Life series. Nevertheless, the arches, columns, thrones, and odd steps, seeming sometimes to crowd the actors to the front edge of the 'stage', suggest a response to a specific influence, perhaps certain Italian paintings, possibly masques or plays. With few exceptions even outdoor scenes take place close to arched gates and buildings. Whatever Barlow's inspiration, his baroque treatment of the simple traditional motifs he worked from produces a series of illustrations crowded with interest.

In the first design (fig. 101), for instance, in which Aesop proves by inducing vomiting that his fellow servants, not he, have eaten their master's figs, Aesop kneels on a step, his master is framed within an arch with columns with Corinthian capitals, the two servants sit at a handsome table, and two tall arched windows fill the remaining space. Irrepressibly, Barlow has his dog walk on the scene, just being himself. The second design (fig. 104), etched by Barlow like the first, is not typical of the series because it lacks most of the baroque elements, except for a pitcher. The background cow, fence, foliage, and crinkly plant relate the Life to the *Fables* series. Uncharacteristically, Barlow felt constrained to draw Aesop largely in profile in order to present a constant image. Still, this scene of Aesop serving fruit to the two priests of Diana, absorbed in their talk, contributes to a sense of action continuing in time, one aspect of his work as an illustrator that goes beyond technical skill.

Barlow's Interpretations

The Aesop of the Life series is not so sensitive a person as he is in the 1666 frontispiece, but Barlow still makes him dignified and intelligent. (Pieter van der Borcht gives Aesop the pointed head that Philipott's text calls for, but Barlow does not.) The rest of the characters are all tall and dignified, and their aquiline features under their turbans and other exotic headgear – sign of the growing

Tho: Dudley. fecit 1678

105) BARLOW, *The Life of Aesop*, 189 × 161 mm.

106) BARLOW, *The Life of Aesop*, 191 × 163 mm.

107) BARLOW, *The Life of Aesop*, 188 × 161 mm.

familiarity with the East – are uniformly serious and benign. The elevated tone of this interpretation does not correspond with Aesop's contrary behaviour; but it does live up to Barlow's vision of the noble book that he was determined to offer the British public.

Aesop's early adventures parallel those of Androcleus and many later non-heroes: a change of masters, difficulties with the wife of his master Xanthus, and a whole series of misunderstandings with his master and his master's guests through his bumptious behaviour and casuistry. In several he appears as a servant waiting on table, which gives Barlow opportunity to draw groups of men and women in gowns with slashed shoulders and the men with headgear to match the women's high-piled coiffures. It also allowed him to draw with care fancy pitchers and decanters and in no. VIII to include a quartet playing trumpets from a balcony above the diners (fig. 105). For variety Aesop stands aside in illustration XII (fig. 106), the episode in which Xanthus has his wife test the insensitivity of a filthy yokel by washing his feet. Barlow masters this unsavoury situation by using the kneeling woman as the centre piece in a tableau of considerable dignity. It is idle to speculate about why Barlow chose to treat the traditional motif of Aesop's exposure of the sleeping wife of Xanthus with gratuitous explicitness. Perhaps it seemed the correct thing to do during the late 1670s, in the full tide of the Restoration court and theatre. Aphra Behn was not at a loss for words to go with it.

Step by step Barlow records Aesop's progress and change of fortunes. Having manoeuvred Xanthus into giving him his freedom at Samos, Aesop imposes his peculiar brand of wisdom on the Samians and solves so many problems for them that they raise a statue to him. In illustration no. XXVI he is shown shaking hands with the jealous Eunus. He is now attired in rich clothing and seated in a throne-like chair beside a decorative four-poster bed on what seems an open-air porch. As in other designs, Barlow's dog adds a catalytic touch of naturalness to this bizarre setting.

Throughout the Life of Aesop series Barlow energizes his designs by the devices he uses in the *Fables* – giving movement and torque to his figures and placing them in different planes in the foreground – but since the climax of the incidents recorded is usually verbal, he cannot always make clear what is going on by action. When, however, Aesop visits Delphi, where the natives have no use for a foreign soothsayer and Aesop's cleverness is of no avail, Barlow suffers no such restraint. In illustration XXX (fig. 107) he shapes the traditional motif into a great Hokusai wave of dark and light Delphian citizens with Aesop, like the breaking surf, pitching headlong over a cliff. It is one of Barlow's most dramatic designs. In XXXI, too late the Delphians also raise a statue to

Aesop. Barlow etched this last illustration, probably, as we have suggested, in order to include Mrs. Behn's tribute to the dead Charles II.

Coming as an afterthought to an already published work with a hundred and ten illustrations, the Life of Aesop series can easily be overlooked. It is second to the *Theophila* series in seriousness and to the *Fables* series in extended accomplishment, but it is still a major contribution to English book illustration. In one sense even more than the *Androcleus* series it is a prototype of the illustrations in English novels of later centuries because it has one central character, a hero, who has much in common with a great many unheroic figures of the English novel, yet who moves in upperclass circles.

Francis Barlow's Influence

After 1687 Barlow illustrated no books. Vertue's remark about 'Cutts for a new edition of Aesop's Fables, in which Undertaking he wanted due Encoragement' implies that the second edition had a disappointing sale. He put together sheets to form issues of the *Aesop's Fables*, as in 1703; ('R. Newcomb for Francis Barlow and are to be sold by the Booksellers of London and Westminster') that have been mistaken for new editions. Then Etiènne Roger's *Les fables d'Esope* (Amsterdam, 1704) shows that Barlow achieved some fame outside Britain in his own day. For this edition Roger, a music publisher, acquired Barlow's plates for the Aesop-and-animals frontispiece (which he used also as the first illustration in the Life), twenty-six of the Life of Aesop episodes, and a hundred and seven of the fables. Some of the impressions are weak and some show fresh graver work. Roger's title-page statement reads: *Avec les Figures dessinées & gravées par F. Barlouw, d'une manière savante & Pittoresque. Ouvrage très-utile aux Peintres, Sculpteurs, Graveurs, & autres Artistes ou Amateurs de Dessein, qui y trouveront des Animaux & des Oiseaux dessinez d'un gout exquis & d'une touche savante.* The tribute to Barlow is the more genuine since his name is on none of the plates. Roger discards Barlow's polyglot text and for an all-English flavour translates L'Estrange's English edition into French, again with acknowledgement. He therefore has to cut off Aphra Behn's engraved text from each of the plates. On the Life of Aesop plates he leaves the top border of the cartouche. The book is an instance of Europe getting its own literature and art on the rebound from England.

Other evidences that Barlow's work was admired on the Continent are the engraved title-page and sixty copied illustrations in Ramoissenet's edition (Paris, 1790?), Augustin Legrand's carefully engraved copies of Barlow's plates for La Fontaine's *Recueil de fables d'Esope et autres mythologistes* (Paris, 1799), and the polyglot *Hundert Fabeln nach Aesop und den grossten Fabelndichtern aller Zeiten* (Berlin,

1830) with a hundred coloured engravings based on Barlow's illustrations.

We have already noted a 1759 deck of cards with designs from 'Aesop's Fables exactly copied after Barlow'. Barlow's designs serve as models for English illustrators of Aesopic fables throughout the eighteenth and nineteenth centuries. Among the English followers of Barlow the first is Elisha Kirkall. He engraved in relief on metal at least eighty-three designs after Barlow among his hundred and ninety-six attractive small oval illustrations for Samuel Croxall's *Fables of Aesop and Others* (1722) (fig. 108). They were reprinted and copied in many later editions. Thomas Bewick's two series of wood-engravings in his *Select Fables* (1784) and *Aesop's Fables* (1818) both imitate Kirkall's designs closely, as well as his white-line technique. One of the patricians among English Aesops is the two-volume edition published by John Stockdale (1793), 'embellished with one hundred and twelve plates' – *i.e.*, with copies of Barlow's complete series of illustrations and two weak substitute title-page vignettes, one drawn by Thomas Stothard. The illustrations, reduced about half, engaged the services of an astonishing number of burin engravers. The plates, printed on separate sheets of soft thin card without captions, reproduce Barlow's etchings with trifling changes in the backgrounds and costumes, some difference in values and spontaneity, but with dedicated faithfulness. They are a handsome tribute to Barlow, though as usual his name is not mentioned, except in an advertisement for Stockdale's books.

The immense popularity of the Croxall text influenced the illustrations in competing nineteenth-century editions even when, as in the Townsend edition with fifty fine wood-engraved illustrations drawn by Harrison Weir and the James edition with a hundred by Sir John Tenniel, the motifs are largely original. Barlow's influence is apparent in the careful realistic drawing of animals and birds and in the expressiveness of their response to their dilemmas. This Barlow tradition still dominates serious Aesopic illustration, as in the work of Stephen Gooden and Agnes Miller Parker, for the strained anthropomorphism of foreign artists such as Gerard ('Grandville') and Doré has had only spasmodic imitation in England.

But the influence of Francis Barlow in English book illustration reaches beyond Aesopic fables and other animal books. In less obvious ways, as we have tried to show, he is the first English artist to understand and practise modern interpretive illustration. Taking his cue from Marcus Gheeraerts the elder, he introduced a naturalistic treatment of characters within their environment, something that his predecessors Francis Cleyn and Wenceslaus Hollar failed to appreciate fully. Like Gheeraerts he left behind the decorative representationalism of the small Italianate woodcuts of Janot, Salomon, De Marnef, Plantin, and Solis from which his Aesop motifs descended. He made his most significant personal contribution in so drawing and organizing his characters that they interact in a dynamic, expressive, and when appropriate dramatic way that is at the heart of interpretive illustration.

Barlow's *Aesop's Fables* is one of the chief English illustrated books. His *Theophila* illustrations by themselves are masterly; few sets of illustrations match them in sensitivity and high seriousness. His *Androcleus* series and his contributions to the *Aesopics* were ruined by inferior etching; yet, viewed through eyes familiar with his original drawings, they add weight to the body of his accomplishment. After that his *Pelecanicidium* and *Severall Wayes of Hunting, Hawking & Fishing* are the most substantial of his miscellaneous books. The list is short, but the volume of individual designs is greater than that of most modern illustrators, and the quality of his draughtsmanship equals that of any English practitioner. He is the honest craftsman more often than he is the worker of the magic at the heart of all great art. Yet since an illustrator cannot be judged simply as an artist, to the volume and quality of his work Francis Barlow adds ability to interpret his texts with revelatory insight that makes him the father of English book illustration.

Aubrey, John.
 Aubrey's Brief Lives.
 O. L. Dick, ed. Penguin, 1962.
Auerbach, Erna.
 'Early English Engravings.'
 Burlington Magazine xciv, Nov. 1952.
Ayrton, Michael.
 British Drawings.
 Collins, 1946.

Baker, C. H. Collins, and Constable, W. G.
 *English Painting of the Sixteenth and
 Seventeenth Centuries.*
 Florence: Pantheon; Paris: Pegasus, n.d.
 [1930].
Benesch, Otto.
 *Artistic and Intellectual Trends from Rubens
 to Daumier: As Shown in Book Illustration.*
 Cambridge, Mass.: Harvard College
 Library, 1943.
Bennett, Edward T.
 The Tower Menagerie.
 R. Jennings, 1829.
Bland, David F.
 A History of Book Illustration.
 Faber & Faber, 1969.
Boner, Ulrich.
 *Der Edelstein. Faksimile der ersten
 Druckausgabe Bamberg 1461.*
 D. Fouquet, ed. Stuttgart: Müller and
 Schindler, n.d. [1972].

*Catalogue of Prints and Drawings in the
 British Museum. Division I. Political and
 Personal Satires.*
 The British Museum, 1873.
Clair, Colin.
 A History of Printing in Great Britain.
 Cassell, 1965.

Clair, Colin.
 A Chronologly of Printing.
 Cassell, 1969.
Clark, William S.
 The Early Irish Stage.
 Oxford University Press, 1955.
Croft-Murray. See Murray.

Dictionary of National Biography.
 L. Stephen and S. Lee, eds.
 Oxford University Press, 1885–.
Dodd, Thomas.
 The Connoisseur's Repertory.
 6 vols. Hurst & Chance, [1825].
Eames, Marian.
 'John Ogilby and His Aesop.'
 Bulletin of the New York Public Library
 65, no. 2, Feb. 1961.
Englefield, W. A. D.
 *The History of the Painter-Stainers Company
 of London.*
 Chapman & Todd, 1923.
Evelyn, John.
 Sculptura.
 J. Crook, 1662.
Evelyn, John.
 Diary and Correspondence.
 4 vols. J. Forster, ed. Bohn, 1859.
Evelyn, John.
 The Diary of John Evelyn.
 6 vols. E. S. de Beer, ed. Oxford
 University Press, 1955.
Ewen, C. L'Estrange
 Lotteries and Sweepstakes.
 Cranton, 1932.
Fagan, Louis.
 *A Descriptive Catalogue of the
 Engraved Work of William Faithorne.*
 Quaritch, 1888.

Guter, Josef.
'Fünfhundert Jahre Fabelillustration.'
Antiquariat xxii, nos. 3, 4, 6, 7, 1972.

Haight, Gordon S.
'The Sources of Quarles' *Emblems*.'
The Library xvi, no. 2, Sept. 1935.

Hake, Henry.
'Some Contemporary Records Relating to
Francis Place.'
*The Tenth Volume of the Walpole Society
1921–1922*.
Oxford: The Walpole Society, 1922.

Handover, P. M.
*Printing in London from 1476 to
Modern Times*.
Allen & Unwin, 1960.

Hargrave, Catherine P.
A History of Playing Cards.
New York: Dover, 1966.

Hind, A. M.
*Wenceslaus Hollar and His Views of
London and Windsor in the Seventeenth Century*.
Lane, 1922.

Hind, A. M.
A History of Engraving & Etching.
New York: Dover, 1963.

Hind, A. M.
*Engraving in England in the Sixteenth and
Seventeenth Centuries*. Part 3: *The reign of
Charles I*.
M. Corbett and M. Norton, eds.
Cambridge University Press, 1964.

Hind, A. M.
An Introduction to a History of Woodcut.
2 vols. New York: Dover, 1963.

Hodnett, Edward.
*Marcus Gheeraerts the Elder of Bruges,
London, and Antwerp*.
Utrecht: Haentjens Dekker & Gumbert,
1971.

Hodnett, Edward.
*English Woodcuts 1480–1535. With
Additions & Corrections*.
Oxford University Press for The
Bibliographical Society, 1973.

Hodnett, Edward.
'Elisha Kirkall *c*. 1682–1742: Master of
Whiteline Engraving in Relief and
Illustrator of Croxall's Aesop.'
The Book Collector, Summer 1976.

Hodnett, Edward.
Aesop in England.
Unpublished typescript.

Hofer, Philip.
'Francis Barlow's Aesop 1666; 1687.'
Harvard Library Bulletin ii, no. 3,
Cambridge, Mass., 1948.

Hollar, Wenceslaus.
Ezop Vaclava Hollara.
M. Novotny, ed. Prague: Sfinx, 1936.
[With four of Hollar's 1665 Ogilby plates.]

Hutter, Heribert.
Drawing: History and Technique.
D. J. S. Thomson, tr. Thames & Hudson,
1968.

Ivins, W. M., Jr.
How Prints Look.
New York: The Metropolitan Museum
of Art, 1943.

Jacobs, Joseph.
The Fables of Aesop.
i. History of the Aesopic Fable;
ii. Caxton's edition. Nutt, 1889.

James, Thomas.
Aesop's Fables. Ill. by John Tenniel.
Murray, 1858.

Jenkins, Harold.
*Edward Benlowes (1602–1676): Biography
of a Minor Poet*.
University of London, Athlone Press,
1952.

Johnson, Alfred Forbes.
*A Catalogue of Engraved and Etched English
Title-Pages*.
Oxford University Press for The
Bibliographical Society, 1934.

Küster, C. L.
*Illustrierte Aesop-Ausgaben des 15. und 16.
Jahrhunderts*.
2 vols. Ph.D. dissertation, University of
Hamburg, 1970.

McKendry, John J.
Aesop: Five Centuries of Illustrated Fables.
New York: The Metropolitan Museum of
Art, 1964.

Mortimer, Ruth.
French 16th Century Books.
2 vols. Cambridge University Press, 1964.

Murray, Edward Croft-.
Decorative Painting in England 1537–1837.
Country Life, 1962.
Murray, Edward Croft-, & Hulton, Paul.
*Catalogue of British Drawings. XVI &
XVII Centuries.*
2 vols. Trustees of the British Museum,
1960. Here abbreviated C-M&H.

Ogilby, John.
The fables of Aesop . . .
(1668). Introd. by E. Miner.
Los Angeles: William Andrews Clark
Memorial Library, 1965.

Pamela, Countess of Onslow.
Clandon Park.
Guildford: Biddles, 1958.
Parthey, Gustav.
*Wenzel Hollar: Beschreibendes
Verzeichniss seiner Kupferstiche.*
Berlin: Nicolaischen Buchhandling.
F. A. Borovsky, 1853–1858.
Erganzungen. Prague: 1898.
Powicke, Sir F. Maurice, and Fryde, E. B.
Handbook of British Chronology.
Royal Historical Society, 1961.

Ray, Anthony.
English Delftware Tiles.
Faber & Faber, 1973.
Reitlinger, Henry.
From Hogarth to Keene.
Methuen, 1938.
Rostenberg, Leona.
*English Publishers in the Graphic Arts
1599–1700.*
New York: Burt Franklin, 1963.

Scheler, Lucien.
'La persistance du motif dans l'illustration
des fables d'Esope du seizième et
dix-septième siècle.'
In *Studia bibliographica in honorem Herman
de la Fontaine Verwey.*
Amsterdam: M. Herzberger, 1966.
Schlumberger, Camille.
Promenade au jardin des fables.
Paris: Berger-Levrault, 1923.
Schreiber Collection.
Catalogue of English Porcelain, Earthenware,

Enamels, &c. [*in*] *the South Kensington
Museum in 1884.*
Eyre & Spottiswoode for HMSO, 1885.
Schuchard, Margret.
*John Ogilby 1600–1676: Lebensbild eines
Gentleman mit vielen Karrieren.*
Hamburg: P. Hartung, 1973.
Schuchard, Margret.
*A Descriptive Bibliography of the Works of
John Ogilby and William Morgan.*
Bern: H. Lang; Frankfurt: P. Lang, 1975.
Sparrow, Walter S.
British Sporting Artists: Barlow to Herring.
John Lane, 1922.
Sparrow, Walter S.
'Francis Barlow, His Country Life and
Field Sports.'
Apollo xix, Jan. 1934.
Sparrow, Walter S.
'Our Earliest Sporting Artist:
Francis Barlow 1626–1704.'
Connoisseur, July 1936.
Stow, John, and Strype, John.
*A Survey of the Cities of London and
Westminster.*
A. Churchill, 1720.

Taylor, Basil.
*Animal Painting in England from Barlow to
Landseer.*
Pelican, 1955.
Thieme, U. and Becker, F.
Algemeines Lexikon der Bildenden Kunstler.
36 vols. Leipzig: Engelmann, 1907–47.
Townsend, George F.
Three Hundred Aesop's Fables.
Ill. by Harrison Weir. Routledge, 1867.
Trevelyan, G. M.
Illustrated English Social History. Vol. 2:
The Age of Shakespeare and the Stuart Period.
Penguin, 1964.

Urzidil, Johannes.
*Wenceslaus Hollar: Der Kupferstecher des
Barock.*
Wien-Leipzig: Passer, 1936.

Van Eerde, Katherine S.
Wenceslaus Hollar: Delineator of His Time.
Charlottesville, Va.: University Press
of Virginia for The Folger Shakespeare
Library, 1970.

Vertue, George.
The Note-Books, vols. 18, 20, 22, 24, 26.
Oxford: Walpole Society, 1930–55.
Voet, Leon.
The Golden Compasses: A History of the House of Plantin-Moretus. 2 vols.
Amsterdam: Vangendt; New York:
Schram; Routledge & Kegan Paul, 1972.
Vulliamy, C. E.
The Onslow Family 1528–1874.
Chapman & Hall, 1953.

Wark, Robert R.
Early British Drawings in the Huntington Collection.

San Marino, Cal.: Henry E. Huntington
Library and Art Gallery, 1969.
Waterhouse, Ellis.
Painting in Britain 1530–1730.
Penguin, 1953.
Whinney, Margaret, and Millar, Oliver.
English Art 1625–1714.
Oxford University Press, 1957.
Witt.
Some British Drawings from the Collection of Sir Robert Witt.
The Arts Council of Great Britain, 1948.
Woodward, John.
Tudor and Stuart Drawings.
Faber & Faber, 1951.

Ashmolean Museum, Oxford 2, 7, 44, 97
Bodleian Library (by permission of the Curators) 10, 13, 14, 16, 17, 23 ,24, 27,
28, 33-36, 43, 45, 47, 49, 51, 53, 55-72, 85, 94-96, 98, 99
British Library (by permission of the British Library Board) 9, 11, 12, 25,
29-32, 37-39, 41, 42, 73, 76
British Museum (by permission of the Trustees) 4, 5, 8, 22, 40,
46, 52, 74, 75
Courtauld Institute Gallery 3
Dulwich College 50, 54
Edinburgh University Library 15
Glasgow University Library (by permission of the Librarian) 18, 19
Herzog – August Bibliothek, Wolfenbüttle 26
National Gallery of Scotland 21
Queen's College, Oxford (by permission of the Provost and Fellows) 48
Tate Gallery 1
Trinity College, Cambridge (by permission of the Master and Fellows) 77-84,
86-93, 100-107
University of London Library (by permission of the Director) 20